XES

WHY CHURCH GIRLS TEND
TO GET IT BACKWARDS
...and how to get it right

XES

WHY CHURCH GIRLS TEND
TO GET IT BACKWARDS

...and how to get it right

JOY MCMILLAN

© 2014 by Joy McMillan
Published by Simply Bloom Productions LLC
Merrill, Michigan
www.simplybloom.org

Printed in the United States of America

Scriptures taken from the Holy Bible, New International Version®,
NIV®. Copyright © 1973, 1978, 1984, 2011 by Biblica, Inc.™
Used by permission of Zondervan. All rights reserved world-
wide.www.zondervan.com The "NIV" and "New International Ver-
sion" are trademarks registered in the United States Patent
and Trademark Office by Biblica, Inc.™

ISBN-13: 978-0692028681

DEDICATION

To the boy who scooped me up,
aided in the reassembly of my heart,
and who always believed I was more
than the sum of my past mistakes.

CONTENTS

PREFACE

Little did I know, when I nervously hit 'Publish' on that post two years ago, that it would fast become the most read article on my blog, and my most requested speaking topic.

What had bubbled up and simmered in my heart for over a year, had finally been typed up, read, reread, edited, and carefully sifted through in a last ditch attempt to make myself sound more socially acceptable than I actually am.

True story.

Had you asked me, 20 years ago, whether I would ever write or talk about sex - other than in a diary or to a best friend – I would have crinkled my nose, curled up my lip at you, and declared without hesitation, "Umm, *no! That's gross.*"

Partly because writing has never been *my* thing. But mostly because I was only 13.

But had you asked me that same question just 2 years later, my response would have been very different. I might have recoiled at the mere mention of the subject. Maybe I would have sat silent, wide-eyed, drawing deep quivering breaths in the hopes that my silence would effectively masquerade as innocence. Maybe you would have recognized the weight of shame in my eyes.

i

If you waited long enough, refusing to fill the awkward void with words, there would most likely have been tears. And snot. And then I would have sought swift refuge beneath the pink floral shield of my duvet.

This book is deeply personal. Not just because it's about the sticky subject of sex. But because it is a piece of *my* story. Rooted in faith and glistening with hope, you should know it is also pockmarked with promiscuity, shame and addiction.

A distorted image of God, and a fractured understanding of sexuality, simply made matters worse.

But, as I am learning with all great love stories, this wild, untamable God we serve likes to push the envelope and woo us considerably further from our pretty little comfort zones than we'd prefer to be.

And so it is with this unexpected adventure.

This book is a product of my struggle, a testimony of His grace, and a celebration of our freedom.

*"Do not fear, for I have redeemed you;
I have summoned you by name; you are mine"*

Isaiah 43:1b

1

CHAPTER

WHAT DOOR?

Once upon a time, in a land far, far away,...

Okay, stop the train. That's not true. These people live *uncomfortably* close by. Anyway, moving right along.

There once was a young bride and groom. Smitten and starry-eyed, their wedding day had arrived and they were, well...as happy as hounds in a hub cap factory.

With vows exchanged and the standard 27 million photos taken, they kissed to the clink of every glass and danced the night away. Hearts full and feet throbbing, they were eager to launch the next chapter of their lives together.

Alone. Decidedly *alone*.

Planning a wedding had been hard work, at least for one of them, and spending the day in the matrimonial spotlight, while glorious, had been even more exhausting. Providing a much needed respite after a day of glitz and adrenaline, the promise of their bridal suite was enough to recharge their batteries through the final inning.

They arrived at the hotel in the wee hours of the morning and, with great expectation, hurriedly checked in and headed to the top floor. The sight that met their eyes when they opened their door, however, was beyond disappointing.

Where were the fresh flowers and chocolate-covered strawberries? Where was the open floor plan and champagne on ice they'd been told about? More importantly, where was that four-poster bed they had spied in the brochure that had triggered hot cheeks and winking all around?

This was not what they had signed up for.

Too exhausted and, let's face it, preoccupied with the possibility of that greatly anticipated horizontal tango (I'm paraphrasing here), they decided to take it up with management in the morning.

After an uncomfortable night on a lumpy pull-out sofa bed in the small, stuffy room, the new husband headed down to the manager's desk to give him a piece of his mind. A refund and explanation were in order.

After listening patiently for several minutes, the desk clerk graciously asked, *"Sir, did you open the door?"*

Aaah, yes. The door.

The *door?*

After sheepishly returning to his room in search of this mysterious door, the husband and his new bride found what they had assumed, in their post-wedding fog, was simply a *closet* door.

Low and behold...*the* door.

They stood speechless at the extravagance that lay before them. A stunningly decorated, sprawling room boasting an array of freshly cut flowers, an overflowing fruit basket, a tray of plump chocolate-covered berries... and the most majestic four-poster bed they had ever laid their eyes on. Not to mention their bodies.

They had spent their wedding night in the congested, awkwardly arranged entranceway to what was actually their rightful room to enjoy.

I love telling this story[1] when I speak because, funny as it may be, it packs a punch. It is simple, and yet the message hits profoundly close to home.

It paints a picture almost as ludicrous as that of a princess, huddled on the doorstep of her castle, with the keys to the kingdom in her pocket.

You see, there is territory that is ours for the taking, but we have to be willing to step into it.

And that's where it gets tricky.

If we're honest - willing to get real and raw with ourselves, in spite of the temporary discomfort - we'll recognize just how often we do this in life. In *marriage*. We can see ourselves right there in their [wedding] shoes, crammed into that little entranceway, feeling disappointed, disconnected, and completely disenchanted with how hard it's become to keep the proverbial spark alive.

What is it about that door that so clearly divides the fizzle from the sizzle?

Making marriage *work* takes effort. I'm not sure anyone would disagree with me on that. But I don't just want a marriage that 'works', and I think it's safe to assume you don't either. We want a marriage that is vibrant, ever growing and deepening in intimacy. A union that bubbles with joy and purpose and *life*.

But a relationship *that* great doesn't just happen.

Marriage is a lot like an escalator...unless you *intentionally* make an effort and do the work to move upwards, you *will* go down. There is no if, and, or but about it.

This holy matrimony thing takes persistence. And courage. And a boatload of forgiveness.

It takes a thousand little choices every single day. Choices that say *unity* is more important than being *right*. It takes intentionally placing the other before oneself, choosing kindness, selflessness, discipline, forgiveness and flexibility...day after day after day.

And then the day after that.

It takes getting up every single time you fall down, or drop the ball, and pressing onward.

It takes surrounding yourself with the right people.

It requires a hefty amount of prayer and patience.

It demands e*xtravagant* grace. And a whole heck of a lot of laughter.

And it takes prioritizing intimacy - physical, spiritual and emotional - and working to cultivate a vibrant, satisfying sex life.

And this is where the door comes in.

The hardest part of developing a Christ-centered, God-honoring marriage isn't *knowing* what to do. It's actually *doing* something with what you already know.

It's much like getting healthy. We all know we have to stop eating Twinkies and cold pizza for breakfast and start moving more than we sit, but taking that head-knowledge and putting some action to it, small as it may be at first, is where the change actually takes place. Knowledge without action is useless. It'll make your marriage stronger as effectively as it'll makes your clothes fit better.

You have got to want what's on the other side of that door enough to move beyond the comfort of the ordinary, into the *extra*-ordinary. It means being willing to lay down the things we may want now, no matter how desperately we may feel we need them, or deserve them, to gain what we want most...an extraordinary marriage.

"Not that I have already obtained all this,
or have already arrived at my goal,
but I press on to take hold of that for which
Christ Jesus took hold of me."

Philippians 3:12

2

CHAPTER

TAKING UP RESIDENCE

What does that door represent in your life? In your marriage?

And what is holding you back?

Sometimes it's ignorance that keeps us out. And sometimes it's fear.

Occasionally I believe we're stuck outside looking in simply because the unknown that looms behind that door sounds too good to be true, too wild and too exciting, that it can't possibly be acceptable. Or appropriate. After all, 'Jehovah Zapper' is watching from a distance and too much fun in the sack might warrant a downgrade on the good-Christian-o-meter.

Maybe you wrestle with finding the common ground between a holy God and a hot bed.

Maybe you're missing out on experiencing this euphoric connection because you've had it drummed into your skull by an overzealous youth pastor that sex is dirty and sinful, and now you struggle with reconciling those rules with the permission slip your marriage certificate has provided.

It's possible you didn't even *know* there *was* a door. That you were actually allowed, let alone *encouraged*, to pursue a ridiculously great sex life. And that the ripple effect throughout your marriage would be beautiful and profound.

Maybe you dragged sexual baggage from a past blemished with promiscuity or abuse into your marriage. Images and memories that burned themselves into your soul quietly slip into bed with you each night, dictating your knee-jerk responses, and making sexual intimacy with your spouse gut-wrenchingly hard.

Maybe you struggle with a medical condition that causes incredible pain during intercourse. You may have given up hope of ever having a "normal" sex life and it's slowly driving a wedge between the sheets.

It may be that you've believed lies about yourself, or your body, and you don't know how to freely offer yourself in confidence to your husband. It's hard to extend love to another flawed human being when you don't know how to love - and accept - your perfectly imperfect self.

Maybe addiction is threatening to devour your marriage from the inside out.

Or maybe you just continue to silence the ache for more in your heart simply because you've settled for hum-drum long enough that upsetting the status quo seems like, well, just too much work.

I won't pretend to know your battles, sweet sister, and I don't know what drew you to these pages, but I do know it is no accident you are here. *For such a time as this.*

I may never know what's going on behind the scenes in your life, behind the closed doors of your marriage, but I do know that the Author of love and intimacy cares deeply for your union, and has a purpose and mission for your marriage more beautiful than you could imagine. He is, after all, an expert at turning our messes into His message...and your marriage carries a unique, powerful message of grace and love to the world around you.

I don't know what it is that has kept you camped out in the entranceway, but I trust God will start to stir things in your heart and spirit, and that as we forge on together, we'll eventually rip that door off its hinges and take up residence in that bridal suite.

Because here's the bottom line : *if we're not intentional about pursuing God's best for our marriages, and grasping the tremendous role intimacy plays in that relationship, what was intended to be deeply enjoyed - a passionate, life-giving love affair... alight with laughter, fiercely protected, and drenched in freedom - becomes a stuffy, awkward thing to be endured.*

We too often rob ourselves of the very thing God intends to bless us with by unintentionally settling in the entranceway to something extraordinary, while trying desperately to convince ourselves that the lackluster mediocrity that surrounds us is enough.

Well, sweet friends, I'm here to tell you that it's not. It's *not* enough to barely survive when we're called - and equipped - to thrive. Jesus didn't die so we could just barely make it through. While the thief came to steal, kill and destroy...He came to bring us *abundant* life. The word "*abundant*," as mentioned in John 10:10, in Greek is "*perissos*"[1], and is translated to mean *so* much life that it literally runs over in excess. It is *more* than we could ever contain.

I want that for my marriage. A *ridiculous* amount of life. I want it desperately enough that I'm willing to hoist up my bridal gown, don my combat boots, and deal with that darn door.

Friend, it's time we stop buying into the lie that good girls shouldn't have incredible sex with their hubbies. Grab a hold of that door handle and move in like a boss.

I am PK (pastor's kid). I am LEOW (law enforcement officer's wife). Hear me *roar*!

It is my prayer that as you work your way through this book, which is about so much more than just sex, that you'll gain a greater understanding of God's plan for your marriage and His heart toward intimacy. And I trust that you'll find the courage to fight with everything in you to start experiencing, and living in, the joy and sweetness God intends for your life.

I realize that this is a sticky subject for many - especially those who grew up in über religious homes - and I would encourage you to postpone knee-jerk responses, lay your weapons aside, to scoop up your sense of humor, and to prayerfully forge ahead with me. I am by no means a theologian, a sex therapist, or a pole-dancing goddess. I'm simply a girl on a mission. And I'd love your company.

Here...allow me to show you the door.

REFLECTION & ACTION:

You've heard it said, "*mind over matter*," and there's a lot of truth in that popular adage. Our minds are more influential in the way we flesh out our daily existence than we realize. The thought-life we entertain flavors much of how we perceive a situation, how we respond to adversity, and how we engage in relationships.

With that being said, what pops into your mind when you hear the word "sex"?

- What emotions are stirred up? Are they predominantly positive, or negative?

- What is it that you *associate* with sex? Is it joy and pleasure, connection and intimacy? Or is it anger, betrayal or violation?

- Does it expose you in a tender, vulnerable way, or in an uncomfortable, fearful way?

- Do you view it as a chore or a burden?

- Is it ever a tool of manipulation and control?

- Does the thought of sex stir up painful memories? Does the idea of intercourse represent physical discomfort and embarrassment?

The lens through which we view sex will color every encounter we experience, no matter how routine and lack-luster it may be. Or how beautiful and holy it may be.

Before you go any further, ask God to give you *His* eyes for this tender subject as we dig in deeper and uncover the heart of the matter.

"Forget the former things;
do not dwell on the past.
See, I am doing a new thing!
Now it springs up; do you not perceive it?"

Isaiah 43:18-19a

3

A LOSING BATTLE

SEX. It's *everywhere*, except where it matters most.

We live in a sexually *saturated* culture, in a day and age where pleasure drives much of what we do and where sensuality is used to sell everything from body wash to automobiles.

...What used to be considered risqué and inappropriate for late night television has become the norm.

...What used to make people blush was found in the centerfold of a magazine, but now is seen plastered on billboards alongside our interstates.

...What had to be hunted for on the internet now shows up in your inbox and on your phone for free.

But here is what scares me most. It's clamor vs. *silence*.

World: "*RRAAAOOORRGH!*"

Church: (crickets chirping)

When the only voice we hear is the sordid, perverted one of the world, where sexuality is mercilessly exploited by the media and forced in our faces by every advertising outlet, *we lose the battle*. We, the people of faith, who ache to tell our broken communities that God is the author of passion and purity, lose the battle.

Because we didn't even show up to the fight.

We inhabit a sexually wounded world where far more people than we realize battle the demons of abuse, molestation, abortion and addiction. *Alone*. Because they've learned to associate exposure with abandonment, and the church with judgment.

You see, whoever speaks louder and more confidently - whether credible or not - becomes the authority on a subject by default.

Our voice of hope and grace and forgiveness and new beginnings is so desperately needed in this broken world.

So why on earth has the church remained mum on the topic?

It's as if we think God was caught off guard by how fantastic sex turned out to feel, and seeing back-peddling just isn't in His nature, He left it here for us to practice the art of avoidance on. Like we do with mosquitos and the flu.

We have become a significant part of the problem, simply by allowing a false sense of modesty to steal our voice.

The Christian community, by and large, has lost its credibility because it has refused to touch the subject. God forbid we offend someone, or cause the hormonally charged teenagers to stumble by admitting that even Christians have nerve endings in their Southern parts.

I believe we've bought into the lie that it's "*those heathens*" that get to have the fun, creative sex, while we, the prim and proper church folks, get relegated to the 'missionary position' {pun absolutely intended}. While the world enjoys a T-bone steak, we cling to our dry bone, singing "It Is Well with My Soul," while trying to muffle the ache for more in our souls.

We try desperately to convince ourselves that our sexual 'lot' - the boring, predictable, two dimensional leftovers - are God's best for us.

And in doing so, we've allowed our sex lives to slip down the tube, unnoticed and undiscussed, as though they're *not* the magnificent gifts – and powerful weapons – they are.

Oh, how horribly backwards we've allowed this to become.

Sweet friend, it's time to mount our soap-boxes and speak up.

Guess what, world...SEX *is* AWESOME. SEX *does* ROCK. It IS fun and refreshing and powerful, you're *right*!

But it's because *God* created it that way for us to *enjoy*.

Because GOD. LOVES. SEX.

Okay. Breathe in. Breathe out.

Sorry, I get a little excited about this subject. And then apparently I yell at people in capitals. Pardon me.

If we don't join the conversation - bravely and passionately - the world remains the authority on the topic. And considering it was our dad (you know, our heavenly Father) who came up with this concept in the first place, shouldn't we be informed and have the competence and courage to speak boldly on the subject?

We should be talking as loudly, if not *louder than the world*, about this *mysterious* gift that God gave his most beloved creation, mankind. Sex is mind-blowingly incredible...and it's because *God made it that way*. On *purpose*.

God intended for the marriage bed to be a place of toe-curling, kick-the-nightstand-over sex. A place of madly passionate, deliciously intimate connectedness for a husband and wife.

So why do we settle for so much less?

BEHIND THE CURTAIN

Okay, let's get real up in here. No one really *wants* to admit that their sex life stinks, especially not to the general public. Or even if it doesn't stink completely, that it may need some perking up.

And I get that. But where are the book clubs and church groups dedicated to working through and enhancing intimacy within marriage. Where do we go to bare our souls, uncover the common obstacles we face, and examine the basics of what makes our lives tick and our beds rock?

This isn't just how she squeezes the toothpaste tube and where he leaves his dirty socks. This is foundational brick and mortar stuff we're dealing with. Or rather, *not* dealing with.

I don't have studies or statistics to back up this statement, but I believe it with everything in me...If every couple mustered the courage, and intentionally took the time, to talk through and work through their sexual baggage and venture out on the long and sometimes painful road to healing, *together* - dare I say - the divorce rate would plummet.

Yes, communication is key. Yes, our emotional and mental health is important. Yes, wise financial management is huge. And yes, prayer is incredibly powerful in marriage.

But what about sex?

Sex is the glue that holds us together. Quite literally sometimes.

One cannot start prioritizing intimacy - with all the layers of loyalty and vulnerability it requires to be deeply satisfying -

and *not* initiate significant improvement on every other level. It's impossible.

What you focus on, develops and grows. What you invest your time and attention on, you get more of. It's a simple life principle.

Try it. Dwell on your husband's weaknesses and be sure to gripe about all the little ways he falls short at home...really amp up the negativity and nagging...and guess what. You'll get a whole heck of a lot more of what you're complaining about.

If you're a smart cookie - and seeing you're reading this book we all know you are (see what I did there?) - you'll throw your energy and effort in the opposite direction, encouraging his heart and focusing on his strengths and victories.

I love the tale of the old Cherokee who was trying to explain to his grandson the battle that goes on within every one of us. *"My son, the battle is between two wolves inside us. One is evil. It is anger, envy, jealousy, sorrow, regret, greed, arrogance, self-pity, resentment, lies. The other is good. It is joy, peace, love, humility, kindness, patience, empathy, compassion, service and truth."*

The grandson thought about it for a minute, and then turning to his grandfather, asked, *"which wolf wins?"*

The old Cherokee simply replied, *"the one you feed."*

And so it is with marriage.

We get to choose. What will we feed? Insecurity, lies, distorted self-worth, unforgiveness, selfishness and addiction?

Or patience, selflessness, transparency, peace, joy, passion, love and grace?

CAN I GET A WITNESS?

It's time to saddle up and speak bold, una-shamed *truth* about the power, purpose and profound impact sexual intimacy – or the *lack thereof* – has on our marriages.

Are you ready?

Let's dissect this sucker.

The marriage relationship was designed to be a beautiful, *tangible expression of God's heart toward His church*; a great love-affair marked by unconditional love, passion, faithfulness, *vibrant* communication and a servant heart.

Andrew Murray describes it this way: "All earthly things are the shadows of heavenly realities - the expression, in created, visible forms, of the invisible glory of God"[1].

Isn't that breathtaking? We get to manifest a unique expression of God's glory simply by being a part of this marriage adventure.

And sex? Sex *is especially dear to God's heart*, and anything dear to His heart, Satan will try to steal, distort and misuse as a weapon against the heart of man[2].

God created sex for oneness; Satan uses it to create division.

God designed sex to produce new life; Satan uses it to bring death.

Sex hasn't *become* incredibly powerful. It always has been. And as John and Stasi Eldredge so succinctly explain in their book, Love and War, "*only something this powerful rouses the enemy to corrupt to such an extreme*"[3]. And corrupt he has. Just read the news.

On second thought, *don't*.

What a devastatingly *destructive* weapon sex has become. At its core, it is lust masquerading as love, unabashedly tainted by greed and selfishness, with a voracious appetite for power and control.

And it often results in a form of addiction.

Let me just be clear when I say, this is *not* the sex I'm calling us to in the pages of this book.

I want to look at the stunningly intimate, life-giving, spirit mingling gift of sex between a husband and wife.

As a side note, I realize that what I'm sharing may not apply to all of you ladies out there. Why, you sexy six percent with sky-high libidos, who are enjoying fabulous sex 5.25 times a week, while giving your man the eyebrow every time you see his half-naked bod, *you...well,* you can just pray for the rest of us, okay?

I realize, too, that there are women who really struggle with sex, not because of a lack of libido or because of the presence of undealt with baggage, but because it's actually incredibly painful, physically. My hubby and I have talked with and prayed for a few couples who've really struggled with this. The wife will literally be in tears because intercourse is so excruciating and she's so frustrated with their inability to connect fully. Whether it's endometriosis, vaginismus, or another form of dyspareunia, these precious women have found the fear and stress that develops in anticipation of sex, because of the pain associated with intercourse, drives an even bigger wedge into their marriage. While this is rare, it is certainly an agonizing reality for some. I trust you know that your situation renders some of this information impractical, so take what you can, and leave the rest. You understand your unique situation better than anyone, and as you pursue health and wholeness - professional help or medical intervention if need be - know that there is always hope on the horizon. And with that being said, I trust you will glean what you can from these pages.

BECAUSE HE USES BROKEN PEOPLE

I believe the thoughts and stories shared in these pages *can* be related to by a great deal of *hurting, confused, dissatisfied* women who have no one to talk to about this uncomfortable topic, but who long for more.

I'm with you, sister.

I didn't set out to write a book about sex because I have it all together in this department. Nor was it written with an undercurrent of pride, "*come now, let me help you with your little problems because of my infinite wisdom and incredible expertise as a sex goddess.*"

Quite the contrary, in fact. It was written from a place of brokenness, after too many years were spent suffocating under the weight of my own unpacked baggage, surrounded by religious misinformation, and gaping sexual wounds. The vision for this book was conceived while wading in those deep places of embarrassment and shame, even though I had no idea what it would look like or whether it would ever see the light of day. My experience has fueled a passion to walk alongside others who have become disenchanted with 'the marriage bed', who long to understand God's heart on the subject, and who are ready to wholeheartedly pursue freedom.

Please understand too that none of this is intended to offend or discourage you. My purpose in researching, exploring and then speaking boldly about sex, within the covenant of marriage, is to:

- **Expose** lies that we have believed about ourselves, our husbands, God, and sex in general
- **Enlighten** you to truths that you may have missed growing up in a stiff-necked, churchy environment where sex wasn't discussed (and often not participated in)
- **Encourage** you to courageously work through your past sexual baggage so you can fully experience freedom between the sheets
- **Equip** you with practical ideas and biblical truth so you can press in and grab hold of the intimacy you were created to enjoy

"I am my beloved's and my beloved is mine..."

Song of Solomon 6:3a

4

CHAPTER

THE GOD OF SEX

While the church has spent many years being decidedly mum on this topic, God most certainly hasn't.

Right from the get-go He was cheering humanity on. As he sprung into action in the beauty of Eden, Adam's first speech went something like this, *"hot mama…flesh of my flesh!"* as he surveyed God's handiwork in creating Eve[1]. He was pleased, God was pleased, there was much pleasing, and all was well with the world.

In Genesis 1:28, God tells Adam and Eve to "*be fruitful, multiply, and replenish the earth.*" This charge was made *before sin had entered the world, while* they were as naked as jay birds, unashamed, and rockin' the garden.

And God declared it *good!*

But sex isn't just about being fruitful and multiplying, contrary to some more conservative opinions in the church. It's also very, *very much* about enjoying each other.

In fact, research shows that there is no reproductive purpose behind the presence of the clitoris on a woman, and it plays no part in urination. Random fact? Not at all! If you believe, like I do, that this Almighty God of ours was intentional about crafting and assembling every intricate little part of our bodies (check out Psalm 139:13-16 if you require convincing), then that must mean that He put it there purely for our pleasure! Like woah. That totally debunks the theory that sex is intended solely for procreation.

And, as if you needed any more reason to believe that Jesus loves us, get this. The head of the penis has around 4,000 nerve endings in it, while - wait for it - the clitoris has over 8,000[2]. Bam. There it is. Case closed. Just a little nugget of information for you to tuck away and then whip out at your next women's Bible study. You're welcome.

Sex is a deliciously precious gift from our heavenly Father, but if we fail to recognize it as that, we'll fail to unwrap it and wholeheartedly enjoy it.

Shannon Ethridge, in her book *The Sexually Confident Wife*, paints the picture perfectly for us by describing a fictitious scenario in which she painstakingly crafts an entire tray of delectable California rolls for her sushi-loving daughter. Leaving them on the top shelf of the fridge with a note that says, "Enjoy! I love you!," she's hurt to discover – after days of them sitting there – that her daughter hasn't even touched them. Upon inquiring, she's told, "*I was afraid you'd judge me if I enjoyed them too much*"[3].

Sure, it's a made up story and sounds a little ludicrous, but she draws a powerful parallel by saying, "*perhaps rather than fear offending God with our sexual expression, we should fear offending God by our lack of it.*"

Enjoying, honoring and getting to intimately know each other is foundational in a God-centered marriage. Which is exactly why, in Deuteronomy 24:5, it gave instructions that "*a newly married man must not be drafted into the army or be given any other official responsibilities. He must be free to spend one year at home, bringing happiness to the wife he has married.*" Now wouldn't that be a bill worth our Legislators fighting for?

Taking it to the next level, we're also plainly told in 1 Corinthians 7:2-5 not to withhold our bodies from our spouses:

"*But because there is so much sexual immorality, each man should have his own wife, and each woman should have her own husband. The husband should fulfill his wife's sexual needs, and the wife should fulfill her husband's needs. The wife gives over her body to her husband, and the husband gives authority over his body to his wife. Do not deprive each other of sexual relations, unless you both agree to refrain from sexual intimacy for a limited time so you can give yourselves more completely to prayer. Afterward, you should come together again so that Satan won't be able to tempt you because of your lack of self-control.*"

Which, in this age of fabulously snarky e-cards, might read: *Go ahead and use sex as a tool of manipulation and punishment tonight. Said no Creator ever.*

Talk about having our self-inflated balloon of pride deflated.

We're informed by Cosmopolitan that meaning is found in pleasure. We're told by therapists to simply walk away when we're not getting our needs met. We're encouraged by the gossip girls at the water cooler to embrace the "*he ain't gettin' none tonight*" motto if a hint of dissatisfaction registers on the self-o-meter. And then there are those zealous church folk who just tell you to put to death those carnal urges seeing sensuality is of the devil anyway.

But here's the scoop. As people who love Jesus, we are

called to a standard of living that flies in the face of the culture we live in. It's *servant* leadership. A life of *sacrifice*.

We're called to give more than is asked of us.

We're told to love our enemies and pray for the people we'd rather punch in the throat.

We're instructed to forgive, whether people deserve it or not.

In essence, we're called to lay down our lives for others, and who better to practice this extravagance on than our husbands?

Rather than using people and pleasure to provide meaning and value in an attempt to satisfy the ache in our hearts for significance, we are urged to press into God and allow Him to refine and mold us into His likeness. Much of this reshaping occurs within the crucible of the marriage covenant, and it's an incredibly effective plan when the back door has been nailed shut. Without the ability to walk out when the going gets tough, we're committed to keep our eyes on the prize and push through the pain.

AN INCOMPLETE PICTURE

Because the Bible speaks out so plainly - and frequently - against adultery, immorality, and the misuse of sex, it's easy for a young Christian to interpret that to mean that sex as a whole is sinful. When we're not taught the 'big picture' of God's intention for human sexuality, it becomes easy to focus on the rules rather than the intended relationship behind them.

Yes, there are firm boundaries placed around the sanctity of the sexual experience, but they're there to protect us, not to spoil our fun. They're established to preserve the safety and security of sexual intimacy within the sanctuary of marriage.

In Christian circles we tend to spurt out the "*sex is bad before marriage"* mantra so readily, without following it up with the *"but when you're married, sex will rock your socks off"* part, that we're preaching a fractured message, and painting an incomplete picture of sex. This image is carried into the marriage bed, where it slowly destroys sexual intimacy.

On their wedding day, a couple who've grown up hearing this anti-sex message, is expected to just flip that switch to *'sex is allowed...we now have a license'*, and they find themselves floundering through those first few years of marriage, silently struggling with what they've always been led to believe: *"God doesn't want you to have sex...and He most certainly doesn't want you to enjoy it!"* Resentment grows as they try to reconcile what they deeply desire in each other, with what they believe God expects of them.

As Dr. James Dobson puts it, *"the marriage ceremony is simply insufficient to reorient one's attitude from 'Thou shalt not' to 'Thou shalt—regularly and with great passion!'"*[4]

On the other end of the spectrum, when we're fed the holy roller rules, without the heart and intent behind them, we find we have no genuine desire to follow them. This is often where teens who grew up in Christian homes get sucked into inappropriate relationships and go hog wild.

We have seen this rules-only principle play out many times already in the few short years we've been parents. If we tell our daughter not to do something, simply because we said so, she's left feeling powerless, having had her free-will ripped from her. Of course there are times that this type of boundary-setting is healthy and necessary, but I think this too easily becomes our MO as parents.

More often than not, when rules are laid down this way, she dances on the edge of obedience because her God-given desire to feel powerful bubbles beneath the surface and remains untapped. But when we take the time to explain the reason behind a rule we've laid down, which flows out of a heart to protect and preserve her, she feels empowered to manage her own freedom[5], and out of that sense of being valued and trusted - and powerful - she will typically make a good choice.

You see, relationship has got to be more important than rules. When you remove the relationship from the rules, you're often left with rebellion. And there's no desire to honor the heart of authority when rebellion is raging.

DYING TO KNOW THE TRUTH

The next generation, along with our very own children, *need* to hear it from *us* that sex is beautiful and powerful, and a profound blessing from God.

When we awkwardly avoid the topic of sex, or keep changing the subject when their curiosity arises – we allow their peers and the media to plant the first seeds – we are no longer a credible source of information on the topic.

But when we paint for our youth a clearer, more accurate picture of God's heart regarding sex, we become the authority on the subject in their young lives.

Laura M. Brotherson, in her book *And They Were Not Ashamed*, writes, *"If you are too embarrassed or too unsure of yourself to teach your children, Satan gains free rein of their hearts and minds. . . . Embarrassment is a particularly effective tool he has found to keep parents from teaching their children eternal truths regarding the sanctity of sexuality."*[6]

I love how my parents set the stage for us four girls. I'll never forget the day my baby sister, who is 9 years younger, grasped the full concept of 'baby making'. She, with utter disgust on her face, counted the Douglas girls on her hand and then reported back with horror..."*you mean you and dad did that 4 times?!?"*

Without skipping a beat, and with her signature 'naughty grin', my mom replied..."oh honey, we do it *all* the time!"

I want that for my kids. To model a delight in our marriage. In our friendship. In our *bedroom*. Because when they know that mom and dad have a great sex life, it speaks of a *passion that's worth waiting for*.

Allow them to believe that sex within marriage is non-existent, and they'll assume they've got to get in as much as possible *before* they tie the knot.

"When parents focus only on premarital chastity and forget about preparing their children for the joys of sexual fulfillment in marriage, their message is skewed to the negative with mostly warnings and consequences rather than filled with the blessings and godly purposes of sex"[7] ~ Dr. James Dobson

SPILL THE BEANS ABOUT THE BIRDS AND BEES

So how can we more accurately paint the picture of marital intimacy? Well, we need to clearly communicate that sex is like manure. Okay, just stick with me on this analogy, okay? It's all about *timing* and *placement*.

Manure is messy, inappropriate and out of place on the living room carpet...but in the vegetable garden? It's deeply enriching and incredibly beneficial. Before marriage, sex is complicated, unwise and messy...but after marriage, while it may be complicated and messy at times, it is always intended to be deeply purposeful, nourishing and *beautiful*.

Well, I suppose that analogy only works so far, seeing sex is quite fabulous on the living room carpet. But you get the point.

Young unmarrieds *need* to hear the *whole* message and it's up to us to flesh it out and talk it up.

Christians should be having the *best, most invigorating, crea-*

tive sex ever.

We've got to stop feeding the lie that "good girls" don't have fabulous sex with their husbands. I strongly believe that it's the overflow of this faulty understanding about God's heart toward sexuality that has many marriages in the church today suffering from a case of pathetic sex. If sex at all. A far cry from the ever-deepening, relational oasis making love was designed to be.

And because no one talks about this, except maybe the Cosmopolitan-reading 'bad girls', marriages suffer in silence.

If not addressed, it's a dangerous dynamic that has the potential to destroy a marriage.

We have watched too many marriages fall apart for one reason or another, but almost every single one can be traced back to a lack of intimacy. It's a *root* issue and roots tend to be unseen. Though out of sight, they are *critical* for survival.

While sex isn't a cure-all, it certainly helps hold us together through storms that would otherwise tear us apart. You see, sex is like glue in marriage. The mortar of the marriage structure. It requires the *ultimate* sacrifice of vulnerability, humility, and *selflessness*. And it *immediately* creates a shift in the 'climate' of your relationship, and ultimately, your home.

We're multifaceted beings, and when our sexual intimacy is thriving, it has a stunning ripple effect into our spiritual and emotional intimacy. And vice versa, when our sexual connection is severed, the other areas suffer. Little is left unaffected when there is a void in this department.

Every 'sweet spot' we've ever found ourselves in, over the past 10 years of marriage, has been accompanied by a great sexual connection. Every rough season we've ever endured in our marriage has lacked this intimacy, for one reason or another. I don't think it's a coincidence.

While it's possible to have great sex without being married, it's virtually impossible to have a great marriage without sex. Yes, great sex can be a purely mechanical encounter that lacks the spirit-mingling, bonding experience of making love to a spouse, but understand that, while there are rare exceptions to this (a medical issue or physical separation), *sex was made for marriage, and marriage for sex.*

When we don't realize the power and influence of sexual intimacy in our marriage - and acknowledge that God designed, ordained and blessed it - we won't fight as fiercely to preserve and nurture it.

We have an enemy who will do everything he can to get us into bed before we get married, and everything he can to keep us out afterwards. Without an honest, courageous voice on the topic, we will continue to lose the next generation of youth to a warped view of sex, and lose the next generation of marriages to a cold bed.

KICKING IT, CHURCH GIRL STYLE

I refuse to be a statistic. I refuse to settle for a lousy sex life in a marriage that barely ticks simply because too many Christians are too bristly to talk about this stuff. I will *not* remain quiet about the need for this conversation to be had within the walls of the church, no matter how many uncomfortable deer-in-the-headlights stares I may receive. I will continue to say "orgasm" and "clitoris" in fellowship halls to sweet little church gals who blush at the mention because I'm sick and tired of this topic being swept under the rug, or kicked to the curb for the world to enjoy. *Enough.*

In the same way the symbol of the rainbow - which used to be a hope-filled sign of God's promise to His people - has now become synonymous with something that instantly raises hackles and brings division, sex has been twisted from its original purpose and has evolved to represent something completely different.

Well, sweet friend, I'm here to declare that it's high time we took it back! You coming?

REFLECTION & ACTION:

- What did your parents teach you, or unintentionally model for you, about sexuality while you were growing up? How did it impact the way you interacted with boys and handled sexually-charged encounters? How does this affect what you want to teach your children on the topic?

- Where have you bought into the lie that Godliness and sexuality were mutually exclusive? Ask God to give you a greater understanding of His heart toward sexual intimacy and to start to bubble a greater excitement in your heart to taste of the depths of true intimacy.

- If you ever wondered how important sex is to God's heart, notice that He dedicated an entire book to its detailed, juicy exploration. Find some time to slip away and read Song of Solomon 2:3-17 and Song of Solomon 4:1-7 with your man. It's steamy stuff!

*"Therefore a man shall leave his father and his mother
and hold fast to his wife,
and they shall become one flesh"*

Genesis 2:24

5

CHAPTER

CHASING EXTRAORDINARY

Some years ago on a hot summers day in south Florida, a little boy decided to go for a swim in the old swimming hole behind his house.

In a hurry to dive into the cool water, he ran out the back door, leaving behind shoes, socks, and shirt, in typical boy fashion. He flew into the water, not realizing that as he swam toward the middle of the lake, an alligator was swimming toward the shore. His mother, who was in the house, looking out the window, saw the two as they got closer and closer together. In utter fear, she ran toward the water, yelling to her son as loudly as she could.

Hearing her voice, the little boy became alarmed and made a U-turn to swim to his mother. But it was too late. Just as he reached her, the alligator reached him.

From the dock, the mother grabbed her little boy by the arms as the alligator latched onto his legs. Thus began an incredible tug-of-war between the two. The alligator was much stronger than the mother, but the mother was much too passionate to let go. A farmer happened to drive by and, hearing her screams, raced from his truck and shot the alligator.

Remarkably, after weeks and weeks in the hospital, the little boy survived. His legs were extremely scarred by the vicious attack of the animal and, on his arms, were deep scratches where his mother's fingernails had dug into his flesh in her effort to hang on to the son she loved.

A newspaper reporter who interviewed the boy after the trauma, asked if he would be willing to show him his scars. The boy lifted his pant legs. And then, with obvious pride, he said to the reporter, "But look at my arms. I have great scars on my arms, too. I have them because my mom wouldn't let go."[1]

We can all identify with the little boy in this story because we all have scars. No, not likely from an alligator attack or anything quite as dramatic, but we carry the scars of a painful past, broken relationships, or a distorted self-image. We carry these into marriage and, together with our spouse's scars, we can become discouraged by the signs of attack all around us.

But we need to remember that some of those unwelcome marks left on our lives, and in our marriages, are there because we have a Heavenly Father who has refused to let us go. Behind *every* scar is a story.

In the same way the unsightly ribbons of white that streak across my belly act as a daily reminder that, at one point in time, my body was too small to contain the life that grew within, my heart bears stretch marks that suggest that it too, at one point, was not large enough to hold all the love my life contains. Marriage has stretched us in ways we could never have imagined. Rather than hide those 'scars' and *pretend* we have it all together, we choose to use them as a humble reminder of how faithful and good our God has been. Through everything we've encountered, He's never let us go.

We are not on this journey alone. We can rest assured that when struggles arise - and they will - that we have a God who will fight on our behalf and, holding us tightly, will bring us out on the other side - stronger and wiser.

He is a faithful provider of 2nd and 5th and 79th chances, of redemption and transformation and renewal in your marriage. There is *always* hope. *Always.* It's His specialty, you see. With that one scandalous act of grace upon a Roman cross, hope became the anchor to our souls, the wings to our spirit, and the force that propels us onward.

He is a constant source of wisdom, strength and guidance. But here's the catch, friend...we need to be willing to look up, press in, and grab hold of it.

LOOK UP

We've lived in the country for almost four years now, and we just *love* it out here in our little neck of the woods. I remember running out to close up the chicken coop late one night and being completely caught off guard by the sky. I had forgotten just how majestic a clear country sky was in the darkest hours of night. Having spent much of my life in or near a large city, with all the streetlights and pollution that come with it, life in the country still feels new to me at times. But there they were, hundreds and thousands of twinkling lights of all different sizes, in varying brightness, filling the heavens above. The glory of it all literally stole my breath.

"God, how did I forget about this?" I whispered, frozen in my tracks, regretting the countless nights I'd gone about my business without so much as a thought to this incandescent canopy. It's here every single night, but I forget to turn my

gaze upward.

And so it is with mankind and marriage. Our ever-present source of comfort and hope waits in the wings, eager to swoop in and breathe life into the dark places, if only we'll invite Him in and relinquish control.

I *want* an extraordinary marriage. I always have. Despite a slew of destructive relationships and a broken engagement, I have always known the kind of marriage I wanted to be a part of. Watching families fall apart, while my parents stood their ground and created a hub of safety and security, firmly cemented this conviction in my heart.

But it doesn't happen by accident. Quite the opposite. It *will not* happen apart from commitment and intentional steps in the right direction.

Cultivating the sort of marriage that will survive the storms of life and thrive in a world at war with itself, one that carries with it a power and influence that can effect generations to come, has meant...

- dealing with the regret and shame of a past blemished with foolishness and promiscuity. It has taken years to peel back the layers, and many more tears than I can count, but it has been so very worth it. I realize I am still very much under construction, but so is my hubby, and sojourning *together* on the road to wholeness has proven to be one of my favorite parts of married life.

- desiring to be the wife God intended me to be. When we recognize that *we* haven't arrived, and that it's good to be learning and evolving, we're able to embrace the process and not fight it. I *want* to be ever-growing, and maturing, and stepping out of my comfort zone. To bless my husband's socks off. And preferably, his pants.

- making an effort to get healthy, to choose the 'best' over the 'good', and to get comfortable in my skin, realizing that I *am* fearfully and wonderfully made. And that, despite the fact that my post-nursing boobs resemble fried eggs on hinges, my husband still finds me ravishing.

- keeping my priorities in check. And keeping the main thing, *the main thing*. One of the greatest gifts I can give my children, is to love their daddy extravagantly. Our children can wait while we work on our marriage - but our marriage *will not* wait while we work on our kids.

- not allowing busyness in *good* things to diminish fruitfulness in the most *important* things. Don't sacrifice your marriage on the altar of good works. Too many leaders have lost their marriages because their ministry or organization became their mistress.

- guarding my heart against the temptation to dwell on my husband's short-comings and inadequacies, rather than focusing on his many good qualities and strengths. Our husbands will live up to what we believe about them...what are you believing about yours?

- doing my part to guard his heart and protect his mind from sexual temptation. A satisfied man has *little* desire to look elsewhere. Notice I said '*little*'...not '*no*'.

- going *out of my way* to keep the spark alive; to smile at, laugh and flirt with, the one my soul loves.

- and it's about constantly putting to death my nagging selfishness to have *my* needs met first.

When you're tempted to look at the unsightly scars on your heart, listen carefully to the love story they tell. Choose to see, not the theme of pain or shame some chapters carry, but the beauty that the big picture represents: steadfastness, resilience, a refusal to give up, determination, and divine back-up.

An extraordinary marriage will always be available to us, not because of anything extra special we bring to the table, but because of the extraordinary God we serve.

"For I know the plans I have for you," says the Lord,
"plans to prosper you and not to harm you,
plans to give you hope and a future"

Jeremiah 29:11

6

CHAPTER

ON PERENNIALS
AND PATIENCE

When we found out, just days before Christmas, that my husband had been assigned to the Saginaw area police post, I was devastated. Apart from being one of the most dangerous cities in the US at the time, this also meant an hour long commute each way, which spelled out an inevitable move.

With an 18 month old, and another on the way, my survival as a stay-at-home mom was directly connected to the support network I'd established around me. The idea of transplanting was gut-wrenching.

I remember looking out of our large living room window at the snow that had been freshly heaped that morning, under which lay 120+ tulip bulbs, and thinking..."*I'm really going to miss these flowers!*" Having been informed, upon closing on that house - our very first home together, that the previous owners had invested over a thousand dollars into their tulip beds, these blooms had fast become one of my favorite things about that property. Even after 5 years in that home, they remained a hope-stirring tool I pulled from my arsenal every time the dreary Michigan winter threatened to swallow my happiness whole.

Spring would *eventually* come, bringing with it more tulips than every vase in my house could accommodate, and gosh darn-it, I was going to survive the winter to reap that harvest.

But now we were being plucked out from everything we knew and I was utterly terrified. Awfully dramatic for a girl who moved halfway across the world 3 times as an insecure teen-ager, I know...but I was hormonal, lonely and exhausted after 5 months of single parenting while my hubby endured police academy. I ached to have our "normal" life back.

As a side note, you should know, I don't have a particularly green thumb. In fact, my older sister once informed me that my house was where plants went to die. Needless to say, low maintenance perennials were my friends.

I would certainly miss that snow-buried promise of spring, and the delight they brought my best friend when, on her birth-day, she received the first clippings. They bloomed just in time to celebrate April 20th, each and every year, and the con-sistency was good for my seasonal-affective-disordered soul.

TRADING SPACES

But God loves me well, and within a year we had moved into a lovely little community an hour north-east. But get this, here's what still amazes me...we moved into a beautiful home that boasted 9 peony bushes that lined the West side of the house, with another 2 growing around the south cor-ner. I was absolutely smitten. God had taken care of the smallest of details and I would once again have the promise of something beautiful to cling to during the gloomy winter months.

Hang tight, friend. You may be wondering what on earth perennials have to do with sex...or maybe you're a linguistic gymnast and you're waiting for me to pull off a fancy word trick, brilliantly turning the word "perennial" into "perineal." Not gonna happen.

But, I *am* headed somewhere with this.

Two years after we had settled in, we started to notice the startling lack of trees on our almost 4 acres, and thought a few more flowering shrubs might be in order as well. We started researching and shopping around for what might flourish best in our area, and I promptly started drooling over the gorgeous sprays of forsythia I kept seeing. Talk about fancy *and* flamboyant!

Our hunt ended when we received a packet in the mail from the Arbor Day Foundation offering us an incredible deal on shrubs, bushes and trees. We went to town ordering crabapples, lilacs, sugar maples, a hawthorn, and a couple of forsythia.

I was giddy at the thought of what would soon arrive on our doorstep. At the sound of every squealing truck brake, I checked the driveway for the FEDEX guy. I could practically smell the scent of Spring blossoms lingering in the air. Those majestic sprays of gold and gorgeous sprigs of pink would soon fill the open spaces of our yard.

I'm sure you can imagine how baffled I was when a cardboard tube arrived in the mail from the Arbor Day Foundation. What an unusual way to ship planting and maintenance information.

Surely they could have simply attached tags to the trees when they arrived on the truck?

My jaw literally dropped when inside the tube we discovered 10 color-coded sticks.

Ta-da, our order had arrived. Yay (imagine sarcastic jazz-hands here).

Apparently these were the 10 trees we had ordered, each marked with a unique color to specify their kind. *You have got to be kidding me,* I thought. These were *not* the lovely plants we were expecting. These were quite literally twigs with roots.

My visions of spring arrangements peppered with long, leggy sprigs of yellow and pink died a sudden death.

After the initial disappointment wore off, a sense of foolishness started to settle in. Did I really think I could score a mature bush or tree for $3.99, no matter how desperately I willed it to be so?

But I *had* expected it. And I continue to expect it...maturity and growth, on the cheap...only to be painfully reminded that it *only* occurs over time, and at a high price.

MAKING PEACE WITH PATIENCE

Walking into marriage 10 years ago I thought I had it pretty much together. I was ready to show off my plumage.

After all, I was raised by parents who still, after 40 years, adore each other and sneak lip-lockage in public...we had taken an extensive premarital course and had unpacked a considerable amount of junk from our proverbial trunks...and we were incredibly blessed to have been surrounded by stunning examples of what a healthy marriage looks like.

But I quickly discovered all I had to offer was a twig. *A stick with some pretty good roots on it.*

Not because those things didn't matter, or had no influence on how we started out our marital journey, but because there are things in life that can *only* be formed over time, developed through trial, forged through fire, nourished and strengthened through rest, and fortified through lonely winters and break-through springs.

I'll be honest. I was a little cocky coming to marriage. Okay, *really* cocky.

We had laid down ground rules for our finances, had established guidelines for how perfectly we would parent our angelic children, had hashed out our 5 step plan to achieve our goals and dreams, and had divvied out the roles and responsibilities involved in doing life together as a couple. We had worked through the bulk of the issues born out of our respective upbringings, and the sexual baggage from my past - while ugly and unexpected - had been talked through.

I was sure to be the happiest little home-makin' bride this side of paradise. We were gonna knock this sucker out of the park!

But then the newlywed intoxication wore off and reality hit. And it hit *hard*.

This gig was serious work and, while we had the basics of "she needs love, he needs respect" down pat, we found ourselves simply going through the motions to avoid conflict, while banging our heads over minor issues and struggling to communicate about deeper matters. Our sex life was dull and awkward, and our hearts were aching for more. We read books, attended conferences, and led marriage classes. But still the gnawing continued. We were being stretched out of our comfort zones, and were forced to face our deepest insecurities.

It turns out that we were experiencing what is commonly referred to as: *"growth."*

And it was uncomfortable. Who knew?

Maturity and a deeper level of intimacy - physical, spiritual and emotional - *always* take time. There are no shortcuts available. Trust me, I've hunted high and low for the 'fast forward' button in a desperate attempt to skip a frame or two, but to no avail.

So as we start to unpack some of the key elements that make up oneness of body, mind & spirit over the next several chapters, I pray that your vision is restored and your hope is renewed as you press into growth.

*"My goal is that they may be encouraged
in heart and united in love,
so that they may have the full riches
of complete understanding,
in order that they may know the mystery
of God, namely Christ,
in whom are hidden all the treasures
of wisdom and knowledge"*

Colossians 2:2-3

7

CHAPTER

BECAUSE MARRIAGE IS JUST HARD

There is a profound and undeniable distinction between *head* knowledge and *experiential* knowledge.

You could study for years, read books and interview people, in order to find out all you could about Tom Hanks...and you'd learn a lot about the man. And space shuttles, deserted islands, and shrimp. You'd most likely watch every one of his movies and assign yourself the role of fan club president, and in the end you will have gained yourself a whole bunch of *head* knowledge.

But experiential knowledge? After 25+ years of marriage, that is Rita Wilson's department.

It is tempting to assume that marriage might be easy if you play your cards correctly early on, take every premarital class you can, read every Happy Marriages for Dummies book you can lay your hands on, and pray until callouses develop on your kneecaps. And don't get me wrong - these things *will* make it *easier*. But nothing will make it *easy*. Because nothing can replace the growth and maturity that is developed *only* through real, raw life fleshed out together. Through thick and thin, in sickness and in health. Through diaper blowouts and arthritis.

God knew what He was doing when He wove together His plan for marriage. You see, this whole covenant thing wasn't designed, as Gary Thomas so aptly puts it in his book *Sacred Marriage*, to make us happy...but rather, to make us *holy*[1].

Life brings struggles, with or without a spouse. Life is tough whether you're married or not. But it is tempting to think, when the going gets tough, that your marriage - or your spouse - is the source of all your trouble.

And in some ways they probably are. It is easy to insulate ourselves from others when it's just us against the world. We're able to keep those people who keep bumping into our 'happy' at a comfortable distance, putting on a pretty front for the world and simply retreating when we've had enough.

But in marriage? We're completely exposed. All the ugliness we're able to hide from others, seeps to the surface.

And while horrifying at first, this is *good*.

In much the same way immense pressure and enough time turns coal into diamonds, marriage has the ability to transform us. While pressing the heck out of us, it brings incredible beauty to the surface.

Marriage refines us like nothing else ever will. Except maybe parenthood. That'll refine the heck out of you too.

DOING THE TIME

It's easy to take a look at the greats of this day and age - or even those of biblical times - and long for the wisdom, position, reputation, character, integrity, skills, leadership (insert your favorite quality here), all the while forgetting the lengths they went to, to gain them. The battles they fought when no one was looking, the hardships they endured, the hell they walked through. Quality is never cheap.

We so badly want the medal, but we don't want to have to run the marathon.

We want to partake in the harvest of ripe fruit, to taste the sweet satisfaction of full growth and development. But the thought of walking through the unknowns of autumn and the dormancy of winter, make the promise of spring and summer feel painfully out of reach.

But it's in these seasons, in the midst of that heart-breaking fall and long, frigid winter, that key growth occurs.

You see, God does some of His best work *behind the scenes,* when no one is watching, and everyone is waiting.

Think of the day you found out you were pregnant. Or maybe the day after, once the initial shock wore off and the reality started to sink in.

That insuppressible joy and bubbling excitement. The mere thought of getting to participate in one of life's greatest miracles - the creating of breath and flesh - made you want to simultaneously pee in your pants and wriggle out of your skin in pure delight.

No, that was just me? Weird.

Life had been conceived, and the promise of unfathomable glee, soft skin and baby breath lingered on the horizon.

And then came the wait. Those early months when nothing felt different, and yet everything did. Had you not shouted it from the rooftops, no one would have even known you were 'with child'. You may have been dry heaving into your trash can at work and nibbling saltine crackers, but Nancy around the corner assumed you ate bad Chinese again.

So it is with life. On the surface we see no progress, no sign of fruitfulness. Maybe the rumblings of change hum low enough for us to sense transition in the air, but the progress we crave, and the breakthrough we ache for, seem to have died a quiet death.

But it is in these moments, sweet one - during the seasons of the *unseen* - that God is developing and nurturing and creating in the deepest parts. In a most profound, intricately beautiful way. As is *His* way.

While hidden from sight, those first few months are critical. We may see no change in our physical appearance, bar our ever-expanding waistline - and I'm not talking about the "cute pregnant" kind of expanding, but the initial "I ate 25 too many jelly-filled donuts, get me my stretchy pants" kind of way. But it's in those early stages that neural tissue and sensory organs are being developed. Miniscule eyelashes and fingernails are forming.

In the midst of that silent in-between, a human takes shape.

Because details - while concealed - are incredibly important. And because beauty is almost always conceived and developed in the secret places of our lives.

While the anticipation darn near kills us, and those final weeks feel like pure torture, any wise momma knows that the longer baby stays in, the more fully developed he is, and the greater his chance of thriving in this world. If you poured over a 'pregnancy week-by-week' journal - at least for your first child, like I did - you'll know that something fundamental and mysterious is taking place within that womb every. single.

moment. Nothing is accidental or coincidental. There is a purpose in the wait.

Sure we want to get our hands on that baby now, but we *know* that growth and development is essential to survival, and it makes the wait all the more bearable.

As we begin to feel the weight of that baby in our pelvis and overall comfort becomes a thing of the past, we are wooed to the finish line by the promise of this gift of new life. And this too tends to be a pattern in life. Growth and development are rarely comfortable.

But God is always more concerned with our *character* than our *comfort*[2].

TRAIL BLAZERS

I love some of the colorful characters we find in Scripture. Their spunk and tenacity. Their integrity and resilience. I love weaving in stories of Ruth and Esther and Joseph and David when I speak, because their lives so stunningly map out the process of growth. The strength of character we see forged in the furnace of adversity. The training and preparation that occurs while in prison. The trust that develops in uncertainty.

Hindsight is a beautiful thing.

We know David became the greatest King of Israel, but how excruciating must those years of waiting and training have been for him, after being anointed the new king of Israel. It may be a matter of chapters from our perspective, but from that moment of declaration to the time David reigned as king over *all* of Israel, 17 long years passed[3].

Joseph had dreams and visions of the position of leadership he would one day hold. But 13 hard, betrayal-filled years passed before those dreams came to fruition[4].

But these were *not* seasons wasted. They were years rich with purpose and potential because behind the scenes there was a God faithfully cultivating in these men all the skills and qualities needed to lead well. What the enemy intended to use to destroy them, literally became their training ground for glory.

During the years Joseph spent in prison, for something of which he was wrongfully accused, he was learning the ins and outs of the Egyptian agricultural and financial systems - all incredibly vital information for leading a nation through 7 years of famine.

God:1, Enemy: 0.

While David was battling bears, giants and babes, God was building a confidence and God-dependent courage in him that would be essential in bringing Israel out of captivity and into greater intimacy with her Creator.

God: 2, Enemy: 0.

The struggles and tragedies these men endured may have seemed arduous and excessive, but those seasons of growth and development were stunningly crafted and extravagantly redeemed, and were integral to the victories we read about today.

They were, after all, training for *reigning*. As are we.

Much like pining for a sunny explosion of forsythia, or a mother's longing for her sweet bundle of babyliciousness, I want to experience the hope and peace of a marriage bubbling with joy and intimacy...now. Actually, yesterday would be nice. We want the *end* result...we just don't want to have to wait and watch it grow through that awkward, gangley phase of random sprigs with 4 1/2 blossoms, or that slightly freaky reptilian phase every embryo hovers in.

I'll take *fully grown* any day of the week.

But maturity won't happen outside of tension any more than germination will occur outside incubation, or development outside the womb.

Character will not develop by accident, and stretching won't occur without growing pains.

But it's worth it, this wait. Press in. When all you see that first spring is 6 little buds, know that how you invest in and nurture your little shrub now, will show in its growth the next spring. When all you feel is indigestion, and the smell of eggs makes you want to hurl, press on. You're making a human, for crying out loud.

Some of God's most incredible masterpieces are painstakingly created behind the curtain.

Our little forsythia twigs are coming along nicely now. Admittedly, even 3 years later, not what I thought I was getting that day in the mail...but they're a profound reminder to be patient with small beginnings, faithful in their nurture, and ever hopeful in their growth.

After all, we never look at babies and resent their inability to get up and run a mile. It takes time to stumble our way through life, and marriage, and intimacy.

But the end result is always worth waiting - and working - for.

"But those who hope in the Lord
will renew their strength.
They will soar on wings like eagles;
they will run and not grow weary,
they will walk and not be faint"

Isaiah 40:31

8

AT NASCAR IN A HORSE-DRAWN CARRIAGE

Several years ago we acquired a second-hand Kirby vacuum, and up until recently, I hated the thing. After all the hype about this brand of dirt-sucker, I wasn't impressed. Apart from the fact that this prehistoric beast weighed a million pounds, actually pushing it across the carpet took every ounce of strength I had. Once I'd mustered the will power to clean the carpets, I had to muster the energy to do it.

If this was a euphoric vacuuming experience, I wasn't buyin' it.

Convinced we'd hit the jackpot with this electric appliance, my hubby wouldn't let me get rid of it, so it sat in the laundry closet while I used the el' cheapo we'd acquired when we first got married. It sucked up *most* of the larger particles, like stray baby socks and fossilized broccoli. Regular dirt and hair, on the other hand, it was not too partial to. Vacuuming was just something I did because that's what good mothers with crawling babies do, not because the carpet actually looked any different once I had completed the chore.

When the old vacuum finally kicked the bucket, I took to whining about the dirty carpets...or whining about the stupid Kirby.

Bewildered by my hatred of this legendary piece of machinery, my hubby staged an intervention.

"I don't get it, babe. It's the easiest thing in the world. Just turn it on, put it into drive, and go."

"Wait! Did you say to put it into drive?" I queried.

"Yeah...this little level here switches it between neutral and drive."

Shut the front door. This thing has a motorcar inside it! Well, look. at. that. Who knew?

This beast was like a small car. I took the handle from him and slid it across the rug with the greatest of ease. In fact, it almost pulled me. Holy powerful dirt-sucker!

My love affair with my Kirby started that very minute. I was smitten.

All this time I had been trying to vacuum our carpets in neutral, heaving and dragging and sighing and groaning, because I'd never noticed that rather important lever down there.

We experience this frustration and fruitless exertion in life when we try to do things without fully understanding how they work. When we don't know what we're working with, the extent of their potential is drastically limited.

Have you figured out yet that I might be talking about body parts?

{sheepishly grinds big toe into freshly vacuumed carpet}

Yes, my friend, it's *that* time. Let's get physical...*physical*.

FAST AND SLOW, HIGH AND LOW

It goes without saying that our bodies are different. *So very, very* different. And while we do comprehend that on many levels, we often don't realize the implication that has in the intimacy department.

It's true what they say, men are indeed like microwaves...hot and ready in a matter of nanoseconds. Satisfying them sexually is relatively uncomplicated, comparable to a blindfolded attempt at 'pin the tail on the donkey' for 3 year olds. The kid sticks the tail on the lower-left quadrant of the paper and everyone hollers, "YEAH! You nailed it!"

Hallelujah for simple satisfaction.

Because women are the sadly infamous slow cooker, and because we can't *both* be complicated. Lord knows *that* wouldn't work well. The extra frustrating thing about being a slow cooker is, not only does it take a long time to heat up, in this era of ever improving, high-tech digital appliances, half the time the buttons are hard to figure out if you've lost the instruction manual, and the digital display is broken. So you've got to spend 10 long minutes fiddling. Twist *this* 37 times, press that, move this lever 52 degrees clockwise, tweak this little button for 12 minutes and then pray it's plugged in properly, because if it's not...dude, you've got to start *all over again*! Probably because while you were trying to heat that puppy up, it was actually busy working on the grocery list for tomorrow.

While I'd like to have some words with God about this startling difference in wiring, I've come to realize that He made us this different *on purpose*!

It takes time and effort, honest communication, and a whopping dose of humor to pull this stuff off! And it just so happens that these are all valuable qualities to cultivate in a marriage.

Jill Renich points out that "*one of the differences between husbands and wives is illustrated by their attitudes toward sex when they are physically tired. Sex is usually the last thing a wife wants when she's tired, but it provides her husband with the relaxation he needs for restoring sleep. Some women prefer sex at night while some men prefer to begin the day with this gratifying experience. Another difference is that after a quarrel a woman looks for words of reconciliation, but a man often looks for sex to heal the breach and restore the oneness with his wife. Someone stated the difference this way: "A man gives love for sex; a woman gives sex for love*"[1].

Not only are our bodies formed and wired differently, but our sex drives are typically light years apart. Men's sex drive is like being at Nascar, it's VROOOOOM, WHIZ, WEEEEEE! from the get go. Women, on the other hand, have a sex drive that moves like a horse-drawn carriage. She moves, but she takes her time and when directed correctly, there's all sorts of magic going on.

In the spirit of being honest and self-effacing, you should know my horse-drawn carriage often gets stuck in traffic. My poor husband actually sat down across from me in my design studio a few months ago and asked, "*do you actually have a libido?*" He said it with a twinkle in his eye, but there was enough concern in his face to communicate how much he missed me, and how he longed to know that I felt it too.

True story, folks. Sad, but true. It is so easy for us as women to get totally enveloped in something urgent or pressing, and forget to carve out time for important things like husbands and sex. The busier we get, the more scattered we feel, and the more scattered we feel, the less we think about sex and the harder it becomes to experience arousal. In fact, it simply slips from our minds during the chaos of the day.

Add to that dynamic the fact that the longer it has been since we've been intimate, and triggered our happy neuro-chemical explosion, the less we desire it. Again, sad, but true.

Our heads engage differently, our bodies engage differently. There really isn't too much that's similar about the way we do sex. And this, my friend, is no accident.

When we first start to engage sexually with someone, the chemicals in our brain get all jazzed up. Our hormones are raging, our heart is pounding, and the mystery of the sexual encounter drives our experience. But flash forward several months, or years, and things can change dramatically. Sometimes for the good, as we get to know our spouse's body - what elicits a response and makes them purr - while discovering more about what makes our own bodies tick. And sometimes for worse, as we fall into routine and out of interest.

What once happened naturally, quickly, and with great passion, now takes initiative, work and more energy than sometimes we feel we have to spare.

NOT ALONE

This is where I fear the church's silence on the topic has really taken its toll. Christian marriages, for many years, have suffered in silence. What *should* be the safest place to talk about sexual intimacy has become the most awkward: the church. In an effort to protect our youth from the media's distorted presentation of sexuality, and to keep unmarried couples pure, we've just stopped talking about it. Sex and the church no longer hold hands. It's just seen as dirty and awkward. So the world snatched it up and has been exploiting it ever since.

When a young couple gets married and have only a very

limited understanding of the gift - and labor - of sex, they find they have no one to come alongside them with wisdom and guidance, so their intimacy fizzles, and eventually their marriage grows cold.

While it can be incredibly discouraging to feel like you're not getting it right, or that sex has become boring or awkward, we have grown in leaps and bounds over the past few years simply because we *refused* to give up.

As my mum always said, "practice makes perfect."

All marriages, and the sexual connection they foster, cycle through seasons and stages. There is very little that's static about life, it is ever-changing, and so it's only natural that our sexuality will be fluid and cyclical as well.

While I'll hit on it briefly in a couple of chapters, there are many excellent books and websites that cater specifically to nurturing sexual intimacy through the early years of transitioning from a couple to a family, all the way through to navigating menopause and the 'golden years'.

In the meantime, I cannot stress enough how helpful it is to read and learn about your bodies *(check out the books and websites in the resource section)*.

In the same way one can heave a Kirby across the living room carpet with incredible difficulty just because they didn't know how to work that little lever (gulp), a women's mysterious body has fabulous little levers and switches that, when one figures out how they work, will transform their lovemaking.

YOUR BED = YOUR PLAYGROUND

Religious folk have a really bad habit of labeling things as black or white, that God left intentionally in the gray. We were created for freedom, and it is in that freedom that our intimacy finds its roots and its wings. But here's the trick of the gray area: what works for one couple, may not work for you. And what feels awkward or inappropriate for the people who sit in the pew behind you, may be one of your favorite tricks in the bedroom. Not that you'd know, seeing church folk don't actually talk about sex. It's purely hypothetical, remember?

The only way to know what you and your husband like, or don't like, is to play and experiment. Shower. Laugh. And repeat, as necessary.

A couple of years ago, while sitting around a dinner table at a wedding reception, surrounded by family and friends, one of my best girlfriends handed me a little 'early anniversary' present. Wrapped in beautiful fabric she cautioned me to open it *under* the table. This incredibly Godly wife and mom had slipped us a vibrating ring and, with a delightful wink, said we could thank her later. There's a good chance we've bought one of these little doo-dads for another couple because, indeed, they are a fun little gadget that makes us giggle - among other things - and adds a touch a spice to our love-making.

Your bed is your playground, and as long as you're being sensitive to your spouse's comfort level, are seeking to bless and satisfy them in the process, not doing anything that's clearly spelled out as sinful (like bringing anyone else into your experience; visually, mentally or in the flesh), and you're not dishonoring each other...just enjoy yourselves!

While talking about your body, what you enjoy and what you don't, can feel really uncomfortable at first, it's important to remember that our husbands are not mind readers, and that they would really like to know how to best satisfy and please their wives. If we don't tell them - and we're not wildly vocal - how on earth will they know? They will thank you for those nuggets of information. And then you'll be thanking them. Repeatedly.

I'm positive I roll my eyes and grunt unattractively during every steamy scene in movies. They're so ridiculous and unrealistic. Who shrieks like that? And have you ever seen the female lead frantically grabbing for tissues, or an old pillow case, because heaven knows the moment she gets up she'll dribble that magic all down her leg. Or better yet, if she doesn't get up, she'll glue her pubic hair to the sheets. Seriously, what's up with that? Sex is messy and clumsy and noisy in a myriad on un-sexy ways, why don't they ever show *that*? Oh, right. Because nobody would watch it. Silly me.

Remember that 4,000 vs. 8,000 nerve endings thing I mentioned earlier? Well, what's the point of having those there if we don't know how to engage them? It seems like a no-brainer, doesn't it, and yet we get all shy and weird guiding or redirecting them. I spent the first few years remaining pretty quiet during foreplay because I was too embarrassed to let him know that he wasn't doing it right. Despite my wanton teenage years (which were always adrenaline fueled and never intimate and tender), I had no idea that the clitoris was such a sneaky little bugger. I just assumed it was like a light switch that needed to be switched on, only mine wasn't working. I assumed it was broken - no doubt zapped by a God who was punishing me for my earlier indiscretion - so I simply resigned myself to the fact that an orgasm was not in my married future.

It's astounding, actually, how many women I've spoken to over the years have shared that sentiment. One friend I spoke to confessed that she hadn't experienced an orgasm in 4 years.

As I gained confidence in the arms of my patient and passionate lover, I learned to say things like "a little to the left," "head a little south, love," "try that a little slower." Awkward, I know, but baby steps in the right directions and guidance my hubby was thankful for. Years of guidance and exploration later and that man knows how to satis-fy!

We also discovered that a pillow tucked here or a slightly different angle there, produced dramatically different, not to mention *faster*, results. Because our bodies are unique, and because there's no standard blue-print for what feels good for everyone, nothing substitutes good old fashioned time spent together naked, exploring, laughing, and communicating.

While on the topic of women and orgasms, and I've had loads of time to ruminate on this subject right here, I can't help but wonder something. If men truly took the time to learn their wives bodies - what makes them purr and what makes them groan - and made bringing them to orgasm their personal mission most *every* time they were intimate, would women be more apt to answer with a resounding, "YES!" the opportunity to make love?

POLLY, PUT THE KETTLE ON

I've realized that the old saying, "sex starts in the kitchen" has a whole lot more to do with that little slow-cooker than I thought. If you don't stop in to switch that sucker on, it won't be smokin' hot by dinner time.

When we stop fighting the fact that it typically takes us longer to become aroused than men, we can learn how to work *with* it.

One of the ways I decided to press the 'start' button early on in the day was to initiate *Project: No More Granny Panties*. I went through my underwear drawer and got rid of all the ug-ly, old undies and replaced them with pretty, sexy prints. All threadbare uglies were evicted in favor of fresh and new. Some were cute and comfy, while others were sexy and see-through. I recruited one of my best friends to join me on this crusade, seeing we frequently talk about our desire to want to be better about initiating sex and carving out time for inti-macy, and I knew she'd be game. One day I got a text from her: *"I just bought you underwear, hope that's not weird."*

I loved that when I went to the loo during the day, the pretty lace would catch my eye and would remind me why I had put them on.

Remember, our greatest sex organ is our brains. As women, it's so important that we incorporate reminders into our busy lives to peak our interest in pursuing our husband's heart - not to mention his body - and the more we do this, the more nat-ural it will become.

If we fail to take initiative and allow our naturally lower libidos (and overly active to-do lists) to dictate the level of intimacy we experience, we may actually start to believe that we don't really enjoy sex.

Before becoming a mom, I rarely watched animated movies. They simply didn't appeal to me, so I avoided them. But then motherhood swept me off my feet and before I knew it was I was drowning in blocks and baby dolls. When our little ones were old enough, we started watching animated movies as a family and when we did, I came away singing their praises, *"why don't I watch these more...I LOVE them!"*

Talk about a paradigm shift. And sex, oddly enough, is a little like this in my head.

We make it out in our minds to be more work than it truly is, so with our limited energy and countless plates spinning, we simply resign ourselves to a relatively sexless life. I realize that sounds pitiful, but it's more common than you may realize. I think we get so caught up in the various roles we play, with all the different hats we wear, sex just slips off our radar.

But then it *does* happen, and it happens well, I find myself singing..."*I LOVE this...why don't we do this more?*"

Sometimes we just need to remind ourselves, "*I'm a sexual creature and I love making love to my husband,*" even if we need to put it into action before we truly realize it.

As I look back at the early years of marriage, I realize just how much brokenness I still carried from my past. Sure, the ugly mess that had bubbled up and exploded 2 months before our wedding had, for the most part, been worked through, but I still had some powerful associations and deep wounds, and our intimacy was suffering because of it.

I had bought into the notion that good Christian folk were relegated to the missionary position, aptly named, of course, partly because it felt "safe," but mostly because I had too many vivid memories attached to any un-missionary position. Anything sexually creative was subsequently labeled "dirty" and going there just wasn't an option. My poor hubby would suggest something fun and out of the ordinary, and I'd shoot it down. Nope, not trying that. That's *bad*. Not that the missionary position was that great, it was just less reminiscent of the regretful places in my mind I was trying desperately to avoid.

As God continued to heal my heart and restore my image of sex - not to mention my image of Him - I started to find my voice. And it just so happen that this little miracle coincided with my hubby figuring out how my body works and let me just say, that man can play me like a fiddle!

What used to take a frustrating 30 minutes, can be accomplished in 5. And where I'd end up in tears, rolling over and saying, *"don't worry about me, nothing works!,"* now there is rarely an encounter that doesn't end with us *both* falling asleep satisfied. Or walking out of the bedroom after "nap time" while our kids have had a date with Netflix, happy and fulfilled.

REPROGRAMMED

I recall, several years ago, struggling with incredibly illicit scenarios that kept scrolling through my head. They had been deposited into my memory bank either through pornography that I'd watched, or situations I'd found myself in. The onslaught was paralyzing as I couldn't seem to block them out and they'd hit me right out of the blue. I mourned the permanence of their presence in my mind, knowing that those memories and images had seared themselves onto my heart.

But as I poured out my heart to God, He showed me a picture of a 35mm camera, chock-a-block full of stills, and as I watched in my mind's eye, He turned the camera over, opened up the back, and pulled out the filmstrip. The moment light flooded in, those images were wiped clear and the spool lay empty.

I will never forget that vision, and I can thankfully say that when a random scene or memory does pop into my mind, rare as it may be, it's gone as quickly as it shows up. My past no longer haunts me, and it no longer robs my marriage of sexual creativity and satisfaction.

I realize that those who have experienced any sort of sexual abuse or trauma, and to whom many of my words may sound trite and irrelevant, may need to seek counseling or pursue inner healing before intercourse can represent anything other than pain or violation. If not worked through, this inner struggle will create a massive chasm in your marriage. When sexual intimacy is hindered, it isn't long before your emotional and spiritual intimacy is affected as well.

I've had to allow God to reprogram my heart and reformat my mind in order to fully embrace the freedom he intends for the marriage bed. When we bring assumptions, associations and baggage between the sheets with us, we rob our sacred union of the full spectrum of creativity intended for our enjoyment.

It's not my place to tell you how to connect in your bed, that's between you two and God. It's *your* marriage. But if I can tell you one thing, it's this: don't make assumptions about what's good, bad, appropriate or dirty based on what you've heard (or not heard) from your stiff-necked, conservative church friends. Chances are, the missionary position is the highlight of their year. Take the question to your Creator and allow Him to answer it for you.

As if the differences between men and women, physically and emotionally, weren't enough, you and your husband will have a way of connecting that is totally unique to *you; your* relationship, schedule and preferences. In the same way no parenting book can tell you exactly how to raise your unique child, no marriage book can tell you what works best between the sheets, nor what the magic number is, frequency wise. Sure, you'll find great tips and tricks that might work wonders. But they might *not*.

You've got to find your own rhythm, and roll with it. And it usually takes a whole lot of time, experimentation, communication, and of course, grace.

One of my best friends raves about middle-of-the-night sex. It happens a lot in their house. Another close friend in a morning person, when it comes to getting cozy with her man. I'm not really a fan of either seeing I can't get over the fact that our mouths always taste like death in the middle of the night and first thing in the morning. No one can tell you when, where and how to have sex. But I *will* tell you this...just *do* it. However, wherever, whenever works best for the two of you.

Find your groove and get rockin'.

THE POWER OF THE PACKAGING

After graduating from high school I landed my first job working for Pier 1 Imports. During my time there I met a fellow South African who walked into the store and greeted me with our signature not-from-England-not-from-Australia-so-where-the-heck-are-you-from accent, and we connected instantly. Apart from our mutual love of our homeland and all things pretty, we suddenly had a new opportunity to brush up on our Afrikaans. While hanging out at her house one afternoon, she invited me to go swimming at their local fitness center. She had a suit I could use and a free pass to get me in, but I assured her it just wasn't going to happen. The frightful amount of hair growing on my lower half would make this excursion an uncomfortable one for everyone involved. Don't worry, she assured me, once I got married, I'd never have to worry about not being prepared in the shaving department again. My legs and bikini line would always be good to go! Here was this gorgeous wife and mom whom I'd shoved up on to the pedestal of Proverbs 31 perfection, and if this was *her* reality, it would be *mine* too. Guaranteed.

Flash forward several years and that conversation haunted me. I resented it. Drowning in the diapers and sleepless nights of young motherhood, I had come to realize that a more accurate description of my reality would be the mysterious Proverbs 32 woman. Something about "*a wife of good hygiene and mental stability, who can find? She leaks her milk into the wee hours of the night, and would hop on the next merchant ship if it meant eating the bread of idleness.*" And so on and so forth.

Actually being able to shave one entire leg during a single shower experience was an accomplishment worth celebrating. Both legs was epic. Bikini line? *Pshh*. Ain't nobody got time for that.

While my armpits get cozy with my razor every single shower, my legs and bikini line are reserved for special occasions. Like days at the beach and anniversaries. And summer.

But does the knowledge that I *don't* have braidable leg hair and a national forest growing out from my panty line make me feel less self-conscious and more sensual? You betcha!

Why? Because as women we were created to appreciate beautiful things, and when we feel beautiful ourselves, we're more apt to offer our beauty to others. More specifically, to our husbands.

When I consistently sport hairy legs and hobbit feet, I'm not likely to slip them out of my blanket and place them in my hubby's lap, being sure to gently grind them into his inner thigh and company. I hide them out of sheer embarrassment. When I feel like I resemble a woodland creature, I tend to keep my limbs to myself.

To take it one step further, scientists have discovered that the female human being is the only species that is actually aroused by her own pheromones[2]. The way we feel about ourselves, and the way we show up on a daily basis in this little world of ours, effects how engaged and involved we will be in the sexual portion of it.

I have to wonder whether, in our attempt to promote modesty and inner-beauty among young women in the church[3], we have unknowingly silenced a God-birthed desire to celebrate beauty in the way we express ourselves *outwardly*? Sure, we shouldn't draw attention to ourselves in inappropriate ways or be a stumbling block to other men in the way we dress, I get *that*. But by not presenting the full picture and the reason behind the instruction (much like the fragmented '*don't have sex*' line we feed our youth before marriage), have we crippled our ability, and our confidence, to freely express that unique expression of the Father's heart?

Look around at creation…the color, the variety, the textures, the smells, the detail…it's a glorious expression of who He is, and it has been intrinsically woven into who we are as women. It's beautiful and powerful and *needed*.

Could it be that, knowing how powerful and influential true beauty is, the church has squelched it rather than celebrate it, and then teach us *how* to funnel it in the right direction; our marriages.

So while I realize this has the potential to ruffle feathers, the 'power of our packaging' is an essential piece of this puzzle, so hang tight, okay?

Remember the early days? We dressed up, made the effort and put time and thought into our appearance, but then over time, as our bellies expanded and baby puke became our signature scent, we let ourselves go a little.

Sloppy becomes the new normal. I can say this only because I gravitate towards it *myself*!

I have to be super intentional and prepared to be properly dressed on the 'average' day. And by properly, I mean 'how I would want to be remembered if I ran into someone important at the store'. And isn't our husband the *most important* person in our lives, anyway? He *should* be.

It never ceases to amaze me what a difference it makes in how I feel about myself when I actually take the time to do my hair, apply a little make-up, put on earrings, and a spritz of perfume. I feel better about myself...and so I carry myself differently. It makes a world of difference in my day. When I run to the grocery store looking like a scrub, I scurry in, run around, avoiding any possible eye-contact or conversation with another human being, and book it home. But if I'm feeling put-together, I enjoy the experience far more. I enjoy feeling pretty, smiling at others, and engaging in friendly conversation with whoever crosses my path.

I've found this to be true of my interaction with my husband too. When I'm feeling like a hot mess, with an emphasis on the 'mess' part, I tend to avoid looking into his eyes and allowing his to linger on me. But believe you me, when I've put thought and time into my presentation, and know I smell good to boot, I'm a completely different person.

This feminine confidence is effervescent in nature, and is incredible contagious.

The way in which we wrap the gift of ourselves has a dramatic effect on how we present ourselves.

It is worth noting too that what we physically pour into our bodies effects the output. Our nutrition - or lack thereof - effects our sex life, not just indirectly through our energy level, but directly through nerve health and hormone balance. Repeat after me: 'zinc is my friend'[4].

I have discovered a direct connection between what I put in my mouth and how I feel. Apart from our basic need for quality nutritional fuel, when I eat like a porker, I *feel* like a porker. When I'm lazy and sedentary, my attitude, energy level and skin reflect it.

But when I'm eating well, being wise about how I fuel my body, getting enough sleep and am being as active as possible, I'm considerably more apt to want to be seen naked, not to mention naked and *moving*.

GO CONFIDENTLY

A few years ago, as I slipped into bed after a quick shower, my hubby confronted me. "*So, umm...why can't I see you naked? I've got a license, you know. Why not show me a little skin?*" I pulled the duvet closer in. I hadn't realized he'd noticed my routine. You know how it goes...woman slips out of clothes while simultaneously slipping behind the shower curtain. It's seamless. Shower on, shower off. Hand slips out, grabs towel, curtain opens to woman tightly encased. From there I'd slip into the closet where I'd get dressed in private. Like a secret agent. I had it down pat.

My husband, on the other hand, would walk around completely uninhibited in his birthday suit for entire minutes before the shower was even turned on, and would linger afterwards, sans fig leaf, while shaving, brushing his teeth, and faffing. It would seem he actually *liked* being naked. And it would seem, I did not. No his body isn't perfect, but he's comfortable, and that's sexy. No my body isn't perfect, but he finds me ravishing. Shouldn't that be enough? He loves all of me, including the parts that have grown and stretched. But as long as my critical eye shreds my confidence by lingering on every stretch-mark, or zeroing in on anything that sags, I deny him the gift of myself. It's a gift I long to offer, but never feel adequate enough to extend to him. I buy into the lie that perfection is the only gift worth giving, and so I withhold the beauty that is mine to give. And nobody wins.

The gray matter that sits between our ears is our greatest sex organ, and the way we see ourselves and then present ourselves, hugely affects our ability to intimately engage at all.

It blesses our husbands when we make an effort to look good. It says, '*I care about you, I love you, and I want to delight you in the way I look!*' Let's once again do what we did before we said 'I do'. Our effort means a lot to them[5].

Believe it or not, we are still in a battle for our husbands' hearts. The phrase '*it's okay to look at the menu as long as you eat at home*' is absolute bollocks. And our husbands know it.

We see Jesus making it crystal clear in the gospel of Matthew that an affair of the mind is still very much an affair[6].

Because of the way in which men are wired and the intensity of their sex drive, it takes incredible restraint to not look at other women. While I'm incredibly blessed to be married to a man who has made a covenant with his eyes[7], it's still up to me to make sure that what's being served up at home is *appetizing*.

Our husbands want to be proud of us, to feel that when other men see us together as a couple, there's that sense of '*oooh, that dude did well in the wife department!*'.

God created men to be visual creatures. Don't bemoan it and whine about it, work with it. And in case it needs to be said...don't be modest behind closed doors. Our husbands *love* being entrusted with the most intimate, brave, wild side of their wives.

Embrace your inner vixen...and for Pete's sake, let her *out* a little more often.

Don't forget that even sexier than our girly figure in the bedroom, is our Godly *confidence* in the bedroom! So let's do what it takes to get comfortable in our skin. When we *feel* sexy...we *are* sexier to our men.

REFLECTION & ACTION:

- With a greater understanding of how your body, libido and arousal functions differently from your husband's, where might you need to let him 'off the hook' for the way he's wired? Could you more easily embrace his amped up sexuality if you knew God made him that way?

- Do you understand that if you struggle to reach orgasm, you're not broken? What steps could you take to learn more about how your body is put together and the way in which it responds to stimulation?

- Set aside some time to play and explore each other's bodies *without* actually engaging in intercourse. Not only is this excellent foreplay, but it's the perfect opportunity to ask each other, "*how does this feel? Is this part of your body really sensitive? Do you prefer a faster, harder touch, or a slower, softer touch?*" Creating space for open conversation in love making will set the tone for future encounters, which will help you meet each other's needs and desires more effectively.

- What little reminder could you incorporate into your day to remind you to think about connecting sexually with your husband? Any undies you might need to toss out?

- Next time you and your hubby are making love, keep your head in the game - whenever your mind wanders to your to-do list or the events of the day - pull it back and stay present in the moment with your man.

- Are there any sexual encounters in your past that are robbing you of the joy of creativity today? Are there any memories that need to be surrendered or positions that need to be redeemed so that you can experience the full spectrum of sexual freedom in your marriage?

- What could you implement into your daily routine that would shift a little more focus on to your outer presentation, making you feel better about yourself, and boosting your confidence in the bedroom?

- In what ways could you initiate sex with your hubby this week?

*"To the pure, all things are pure,
but to those who are corrupted and do not believe,
nothing is pure. In fact, both their minds
and consciences are corrupted"*

Titus 1:15

9

CHAPTER

THE TRUTH ABOUT MEN AND SEX

It had been the most brutal winter we'd ever experienced, and the cabin-fever induced shenanigans were practically bursting from our children's seams. It was a Sunday morning and we'd decided to hit the mall after church to capitalize on the enormous servings of stir-fried veggies & rice, compliments of those friendly folks at Yum! Japan, and allow our squirrels to release some of their pent up energy at the play area located in the center of the mall. When you live in the country, at least 25 minutes from any substantial town, you learn to maximize every trip to the city.

We stood by the entrance to the fully padded slice of heaven as our kids scampered over grapes, slid down cars, balanced on a toothbrush and scaled the television set. But our enjoyment of their play came to a screeching halt as four tweens swept through in typical tween style. Leaping, crashing and body-slamming, they knocked down toddlers and bowled over babies. This place just wasn't designed to cater to their size or energy level, and that fact was clearly stated in the rules posted in the doorway. My blood pressure soared as I scoured the weary faces of parents; someone, somewhere had to register a flicker of embarrassment. Or at least some reluctant child recognition.

Nothing. No one.

I could barely contain my frustration when, for the second time, one of these big kids flew past a barely-walking toddler in an effort to get away from the equally clueless boy who pursued him, sending the wee one face-first into the mat.

My silent fuming bubbled to the surface.

"*Hey!*" I hollered, "*be careful! There are little ones - who are supposed to be in here - that you keep knocking over. Calm your crazy selves down a little!*"

Sucking in slow, deep breaths I continued my visual hunt for the guilty parent, half expecting to get lunged at. For some reason we hate it when other people correct our kids. Especially if it occurs while we're doing something super important like updating our Facebook status or tweeting our weather complaints.

It was a matter of minutes before the two boys were scampering up the chest-high padded wall that surrounded the enclosure. Standing just feet away, I zeroed in on them. "*Do you guys actually have a parent here?*," I queried. No, they respectfully explained, she had dropped them off so she could get a few things done. They assured me that she'd said they could play there, so they were okay. In their little minds, permission had been granted, and play they did!

But before they could leap off, a woman appeared out of the bustling mall crowd and curtly asked them why they were climbing the wall. Without skipping a beat, I turned around and calmly gave her a piece of my momma-bear mind. *"They shouldn't even be in here. This space is reserved for the little kids they keep running over."*

I thought I'd feel better now that my frustration had been verbalized, but my heart broke as she angrily gathered the four of them up, spitting out venomous remarks, and marched off before they even had their shoes back on. She continued her rant as they walked away about how she couldn't even trust them to behave properly and that she would not be bringing them to play back there again.

It was then that it dawned on me; they *weren't* bad kids. This was bad *parenting*. They were simply playing like tweens do, oblivious to the rules posted at the entrance, too absorbed in energy expenditure to notice that the 'thing' they just tripped over was a human. As far as they were concerned, they were obediently keeping within the boundary of the play area as instructed by the authority figure who had left them there.

I felt heart-sick at the thought of how my report to her would influence their treatment for the remainder of the day. I had thrown *them* under the bus!

Talk about remorse. My fury at their reckless behavior had immediately shifted when I stepped out of the moment long enough to see the big picture. It quickly took aim in the direction of the delinquent adult. Sure, she may have had a good reason for ditching four 8 through 12 year olds in a toddler's play place at the mall, but when she returned, shopping bags and bad attitude in tow, little else mattered.

How often I direct my frustration and disappointment in my husband's direction because of what I consider to be a rotten attitude, when I have played a leading role in helping him get there.

In fact, have you ever notice the connection between your husband's ability to be fully engaged and enjoy friendly conversation with you, and the length of time it's been since you last made love?

It's wild, isn't it?

I don't know what took me so long to recognize the connection...but it's mind-blowing.

My hackles go up and I get defensive, carefully thought out verbal missiles on the ready. It's usually in hindsight, while sifting through the rubble, that I realize that the poor man has been shuffled to the bottom of my to-do list and is feeling frustrated and resentful due to my lack of attention. Or *action*. It's no wonder he's a crab. I helped *create* this 'monster'.

Don't misunderstand me. I'm not making excuses for them, and I'm not saying that every bad behavior or stinky attitude our husbands entertain is our fault because we didn't 'put out'. That's not *at all* what I'm saying. But, I do think it's important that we own the role we play in this mystery, when basic physical and emotional needs remain unmet by the very person who is committed to meet them.

We can fight this reality with indignation and pride, or embrace it with humility and use it to our advantage.

You see, while we're painfully aware of the overwhelming *physical* need men have for sex, we often don't realize that their sex drive is *intricately* connected to their ability to feel like a *'real man'*, and so it's *something they crave on many levels*[1].

WHEN IT'S TIME TO PUT ON YOUR BIG GIRL PANTIES

We tend to undermine and underestimate their overwhelming *emotional* need for sex. While they may not express it the same way we do – that level of heart-naked-communication does not come naturally to men - our husbands struggle with deep feelings of inadequacy and insecurity. As Shaunti Feldhahn explains in her book, *For Women Only*, making love makes them feel desired, it improves their confidence and self-esteem, and boosts their well-being and performance in every area[1].

Jill Renich puts it this way, *"to a man, sex is the most meaningful demonstration of love and self-worth. A husband's gift of sexual pleasure is full of meaning. It's a part of his own deepest person. How his wife receives him has a much more profound effect on him than most women realize. To receive him with joy and to share sexual pleasure builds into him a sense of being worthy, desirable and acceptable. To reject him, to tolerate him and to put him off as unimportant tears at the very center of his self-esteem"[2].*

When we realize that our husband's desire for connecting with us intimately goes deeper than a superficial, physical need for release, we may be more inclined to bless his heart by pursuing his body.

MORE THAN A WILLING BODY

I chuckle when I think back to our first few years of marriage and recall how arrogant I was when it came to our sex life. I was awkward and insecure, yes, but oddly prideful. I had made a personal commitment to not turn my husband down, and I can actually count on one hand the number of times I have told him "no" in 10 years.

But, before you roll your eyes, gag a little, or think I'm more awesome than I am, you've got to understand something.

A couple of years into our marriage, we had a tearful, snotty conversation about our intimacy. Or lack thereof. Turns out my fierce commitment to not put the kibosh on his advances was just not enough.

You see, he didn't just want a willing and *compliant* body... he longed for an involved, engaged partner in passion.

I had naively assumed that as long as I was making my body available to him, despite its unimpressive wet noodle resemblance, that I would reach 'Rockstar Wife' status by default.

Not so. Apparently our husbands don't *just* want to be satisfied sexually...they need to feel desired, needed and *wanted*. What a concept.

A survey Shaunti Feldhahn took for her book revealed that even if men were getting all the sex they wanted, *three out of four men would still feel empty if their wife wasn't both engaged and satisfied*. This discovery just blew me away and blessed my socks off at the same time. This is not the type of sexual thinking we tend to associate with men[1].

This level of intimacy doesn't happen by accident. It requires that we remain fully present in the moment with them (not mentally sketching up tomorrow's to-do list), intentionality being active in the passion, and on occasion, creatively being the initiator.

I am *still* working on *initiating* intimacy more and tangibly expressing my love for him in a language he is ridiculously fluent in. It doesn't come naturally for most women, but what an *incredible* change I see in our *friendship* when I'm succeeding in this area!

So, slip a bookmark in, slip into something more comfortable (bare skin works well here), and go seduce your husband.

I'll wait...

(cue the smooth jazz)

Welcome back! Now wasn't *that* invigorating?!

Straight shooter, Dr. Laura Schlessinger, puts it this way...

"Men need validation. When they come into the world they are born of women and getting their validation from mommy is the beginning of needing it from a woman. And when the wife does not focus in on the needs and the feelings, sexually, personally to make him feel like a man, to make him feel like a success, to make him feel like a hero, he's very susceptible to the charms of some other woman making him feel what he needs. And these days women don't spend a lot of time thinking about how they can give a man what they need... I hold women responsible for tossing out perfectly good men by not treating them with the love and kindness and respect and attention they need."[3]

Ouch. She hit the nail on the head.

ON TAKING THOSE BIG GIRL PANTIES OFF

Do we fully grasp, as wives, that when we said 'I do', we were committing to be our husband's sole source of sexual satisfaction for the extent of our lives together. Sure, *unhealthy* counterfeits will always threaten to creep in and usurp our role, *but the responsibility to meet those God-given needs lies fully in our capable hands.* And vice versa.

Maybe that's hard for you to hear. I understand that what I'm presenting here flies in the face of this society's egocentric mantra of *convenience and pleasure*, but I would urge you to stick with me and press through the knee-jerk response to disengage and throw in the towel. Or to donate this book to the library on your way to work tomorrow.

Life is full of struggle, discomfort and sacrifice. It always will be. But we can choose where to engage in battle, how long to fight, and what to sacrifice. I'd rather lay down my baggage and temporary comfort, than sacrifice my marriage on the altar of pride or apathy.

I realize that If your husband has been unfaithful, or struggles with pornography addiction, this notion of being their sole source of satisfaction is particularly hard to buy into because it hasn't been the case in your marriage. My heart breaks for you, sweet sister. The wound of betrayal is deep, and aches like none other. While I haven't personally experienced this heart-ache, I have walked alongside a few friends who have.

I was talking to a small group of women on this very topic last year and, for the first time ever in the ten years I've been speaking, practically got booed. In hindsight, the evening had not been well planned. I had failed to glean some vital information - whether the women *really* knew what I'd be talking about, and whether the audience was a predominantly faith-based group. I have discovered that giving a 'God's heart on sex' talk to a bunch of women who don't really care what God's heart is on the matter, is like giving a 'cholesterol is bad' speech at a Butter Lover's convention. I've also found that if they're not mentally and emotionally prepared for a download on this touchy subject, their walls go up faster than you can say "g-spot."

It probably didn't help that this particular group, who were *not* primarily a Christian group, were told I was coming to give a "spicy sex talk." To Christians, this would be accurate. Mostly because the majority of Christians don't talk about sex. Say *"orgasm"* and you instantly increase the room temperature by 10 degrees.

But when those who don't share our convictions hear "spicy sex talk," they eagerly expect toys and thongs and product demonstrations. With illustrations. Needless to say, my talk went over like a lead balloon, and when I mentioned that God intended for us to be our husband's sole source of sexual satisfaction - and vice versa - the two women right in front, who'd been sitting with arms folded across their chests, eyes firing darts, laughed out loud. Like, obnoxiously 'this-woman-is-talking-twaddle" *out loud*. Along with other random comments about the benefits of porn use, the tension in the room was tangible. It was a trainwreck.

It took everything in me to not start talking about unicorns and rainbows, toss out a handful of skittles, and make a run for the door.

I knew, without them needing to spell it out, that faithfulness and loyalty were a luxury in marriage not experienced by these women. In situations like these, yes, absolutely, what I said was laughable. And it broke my heart, once I was over feeling humiliated.

But just because it hasn't been your reality, doesn't mean that it isn't God's plan for your marriage. And just because this hasn't been your experience thus far, doesn't mean it cannot be true of your marriage in the future.

There are many reasons and seasons behind the shifting of our sexual connection with our husbands. On occasion, a sexual ceasefire is necessary due to blatant unfaithfulness, and this may be the wisest thing you can do as you work through counseling and rebuild trust. But in reality, most of the time there's a disconnect it's because one or both of us have gotten busy, tired, distracted, lazy, or quite frankly, selfish.

I think sometimes we're a little naive about the impact a broken sexual connection has on our marriage. While our men cannot comprehend it, it is actually possible for us to go entire minutes at a time and *not* think about sex. Then throw in a few small children that need to be fed and clothed every. *single.* day. Add work deadlines, home management, and the myriad of other plates we spin, and it's no wonder sex doesn't feature at the top of our list of priorities.

But Scripture is pretty clear about the importance of making sure we do prioritize it. In 1 Corinthians 7:4-5 it says, "*The wife does not have authority over her own body but yields it to her husband. In the same way, the husband does not have authority over his own body but yields it to his wife. Do not deprive each other except perhaps by mutual consent and for a time, so that you may devote yourselves to prayer. Then come together again so that Satan will not tempt you because of your lack of self-control.*"

Unfortunately, Paul doesn't mince his words, and whatever 'out' we think we may have is debunked. Unless of course you've taken to an intense season of prayer without letting your husband in on it...in which case, listen closely, and you may just hear God whisper..."*go jump your husband, for Pete's sake.*" In more Godly verbiage, of course.

In light of this commission, and with the understanding that sex plays an integral role in our husband's well-being, it seems inconsiderate and, dare I say it, unchristlike, to withhold this gift from them.

Strong words, I know. But if we refuse to do our part, there will always be another eager to fill our shoes.

Our men no longer need to go looking for opportunities to sin sexually – it literally knocks at their door several times a day. We have the incredible ability, power and honor, to help guard their hearts and minds in this fight.

Rather than fight with them, we have got to learn to fight *for* them.

In case you need a little extra motivation to seduce your hubby tonight? Check out these benefits to regular sexual intimacy, as documented by Dr. Daniel Amen in his book, Sex on the Brain, "Seminal fluid contains dopamine, norepineph-

rine, oxytocin, vasopressin, testosterone and estrogen…all incredible hormones or neurotransmitters known to either enhance brain function, heart health, mood, fitness level, immunity, restfulness of sleep, it helps ease pain, improves bladder control, creates more regular menstrual cycles, has an antidepressant effect, and boosts overall health and longevity"[4].

Isn't that brilliant? How sweet of God to actually load semen with goodies beneficial to our health as women. In case you're wondering, as my mum did when I mentioned this little tidbit to her, how exactly all this good stuff gets into our system (and hey, it's a valid question)…it actually gets absorbed into the body through the vaginal wall.

A TOXIC COCKTAIL

It's amazing how often we put off meeting our men's needs until we feel 'primed'. And while it seems natural – after all, it's really hard to be sexually vulnerable with someone you don't feel you're emotionally connected to – we're basically declaring, *"fill my (emotional intimacy) tank…even if you're running on the fumes of an oil rag…and only then will I consider filling your (physical intimacy) tank."*

Me first. You second.

A wise friend cautioned me, somewhat in jest, before our wedding day that this glorious event in my life was about to reveal just how selfish I was. *"You'll never know how truly selfish you are…until you're married,"* she said with a wink.

And girl, how *right* she was.

I *often* struggle with selfishness in everyday things, but the way I think about and respond to my husband sexually has exposed the depth of this cancerous heart issue.

It's so easy to become inward focused, like an obnoxious ingrown toenail, where our wants, desires and needs become our sole focus and the motivation behind everything we do and pursue. What makes it even easier is that the world promotes this type of thinking as normal and healthy. We're told that this is the way successful people think. It has become all about *our* happiness and satisfaction, and if something gets in the way of that, extract it.

Now, I'm all about personal development and growth, but this philosophy flies in the face of the very foundation of our faith: *put selfish ambition to death, love your enemies, put others ahead of yourself, and serve them wholeheartedly.*

It's about *sacrifice*, for this is the very essence of our spiritual DNA.

What an incredibly counter-cultural way to function. It doesn't come naturally to us, so if we don't go out of our way to live this way, we won't. Plain and simple.

If I'm running on empty, the last thing I want to do is "meet another need." The problem is that my mind doesn't typically stay there. It may linger for a moment on self-pity, but it quickly migrates to an uglier place where it ruminates on anything my husband has failed to do for me in the past few weeks, or all the ways our marriage is out of whack. It's a toxic cocktail of self-absorption and negativity.

It's times like this that I have to stop and remind myself of Luke 6:38, where we're invited to "*give, and it will be given to you. A good measure, pressed down, shaken together and running over, will be poured into your lap. For with the measure you use, it will be measured to you.*"

While this verse is most often used to encourage generosity in financial giving, it's also very much about giving of ourselves. Even when we feel we might have nothing left to give. While it may not be our husbands who fill our tanks back up, God is so faithful to honor these small acts of obedience.

Often, as women, our interest in sex bubbles up *after* we take action in that direction. If we wait until we're aroused, we may just be waiting a while. And if we wait until our schedules *and* our legs are open, well...don't wait up, sweetie.

In fact, while writing this book, during the most intense six weeks of writing I've ever experienced in my life, where all I could think about was *writing* about sex, my husband prodded me on his way to bed, *"could you stop writing about sex and actually come and do it?"*

He knew I wouldn't be coming to bed for hours as I was on a roll, and had written into the wee hours of the morning repeatedly that week. I was beginning to suffer the cross-eyed consequences, complete with stiff neck and pounding head. My mind was so wrapped up in this project that extracting myself from it seemed painful at times, even if just to practice the very thing I'd been preaching about in these pages. *Ouch.*

'Fake it till you make it' takes on a whole new meaning here. When we step out and initiate intimacy, even when we're not feeling 'in the mood', our feelings will follow our actions. We're a little like the hand-dryers at the mall. Put your hands out and you'll trigger them. We're motion activated. Get into motion and watch your interest get activated. Sadly, just like those temperamental little buggers on the bathroom wall, if there's too much going on, we get overstimulated and don't switch on. Go figure.

When I'm feeling tuckered out and resentful of the neediness all around me, I tend to turn inward for self-preservation, rather than extend outward in an expression of love. When I'm stuck in this lonely place, it's helpful to ask myself: *"what am I doing (physically) to motivate his (emotional) love?"*

We crave that emotional connection and sex has the power to unlock our men's emotions. The good news is, ladies: we're the ones holding the key!

It often takes focusing on the depth of love described for us in 1 Corinthians 13:4-7 to correct my heart. We're called to extend this extravagant, no-holds-barred love to our husbands, in the same way it was *first* offered to us: in the midst of our sin and rebellion.

When I lay down self and meet his needs first – even when my tank is feeling empty – he is *passionate* about meeting my needs. It initiates a *revitalizing cycle of service and intimacy* in my marriage.

OXYTOCIN'S SECRET SUPER POWER

If ever you've doubted God's brilliance between the sheets, this will confirm the fact that He likes to show off:

"At any given time, the female brain contains up to ten times more oxytocin than the male brain. Oxytocin is the bonding chemical that creates feelings of affection and empathy. You want to know why women tend to be more invested in close relationships than men? Oxytocin is one of the reasons.

There's only one time in human experience when the husband's level of oxytocin begins to approach that of his wife's: immediately following an act of sexual intimacy. A man's brain literally re-bonds with his spouse, making him, at that moment, more committed to his family, more satisfied with his wife, more invested in his home. Wives, why do your husbands want sex with you so often (whether they know this is the reason or not)? It's because they never feel closer to you than immediately following that encounter."[5]

The calming effect of oxytocin also explains why many men want to roll over and go to sleep right after sex.

Another fascinating little fact about oxytocin is this: because of the influx of this hormone during physical and emotional intimacy, and the cascade effect it has on us, the more sex women *have*...the more sex we *want*. And the same is true on the other end of the spectrum, the *less* we have, the *less* we want[6]. So let's *hop* to it and make this effect work in our favor!

THE POWER OF TOUCH

A couple of years ago, during a heart-to-heart, my hubby reluctantly whispered... "*please touch me, honey...you don't touch me anymore.*" I felt like he'd knocked the wind out of my sails. Honestly, I was shocked. I felt as though I was *constantly* touching others affectionately, and just assumed he was included in the daily outpouring. But as it turns out, my poor hubby wasn't one of the lucky ones. I had *no* idea what an issue this was for him.

It is of utmost importance that we learn our husband's love languages...and become fluent in them!

I don't want my husband to constantly be getting my left-overs. He *needs* to be prioritized. This is an incredibly important lesson I'm teaching my children: God first, *marriage second*, family third. It will influence how they prioritize their own adult lives one day.

I can *say* that my marriage is important, but my actions will *always* speak louder than my words.

Yes, I know, it's *impossible* to meet *everyone's* needs during the season of having little ones at home and underfoot, but it's also easy to forfeit my relationship with my husband in my pursuit of 'supermom' status. It *isn't* easy to go from spit-up covered, yoga-pant clad mama...to sex kitten, at least not without a whole lot of time, energy, under-eye concealer and Spanx assistance. We're exhausted, over-stimulated, overwhelmed, semi-smothered and struggling with our self-image, but like with any fire...if we don't tend to the wood and pay attention to the flame, we'll *be left with ash*.

And we're aiming for *smokin' hot* monogamy, remember?[7]

It's critical that we start to understand that, along with our physical differences, comes a male's unique approach to the value of sex, and its subsequent urgency.

In *For Women Only*, Shaunti Feldhahn draws a parallel between the *emotional trauma that would occur in your heart if your hubby were to suddenly stop communicating with you, and the trauma he would experience if you were to withdraw sexually from him. It creates the same type of chasm, relationally, and is very harmful to the trust and intimacy of your marriage.* [1]

As I mentioned in the previous chapter, we don't have to *understand* our husband's greater desire and need for sex, but honoring it would benefit us greatly. Especially seeing it was placed there by God. So if you feel the need, don't gripe to your husband about his relentless pursuit of your body...talk to the One who made him.

HEARTS AND HAPPY PLACES

I find that when I'm feeling sexually disconnected from my hubby for some reason or another, I disconnect from him in other areas too. Conversation becomes shallow, hugs are brief, kisses abrupt and eye-contact skirted. Not because I don't value those daily points of contact, but because I fear – ridiculous as it may sound - that if indulged in, they will wrongly communicate that I'm *'in the mood' for something more*. The very connectedness I'm aching for gets lost in the shuffle of my avoidance, while my relationship with my man gets progressively more awkward. The longer it's been since we were intimate, the more awkward it gets. The tension hangs thickly in the air. I seem to forget that what I crave will more readily spill out as our sexual connection is nurtured, and that as I allow those non-sexual, emotional connections to be made, the more interested in sex I'll become. How easy it would be for me to simply put words to my concerns, and feet to my belief that intimacy is far more relationally catalytic than we realize.

In talking about the importance of meeting his need for physical intimacy, which then motivates a desire in him to meet our need for emotional intimacy, I would be *remiss* to not mention the wisdom and importance of a man intentionally choosing to touch his wife's heart *first*. It triggers the same cycle. The longer I live this married life the more I realize that it's about *both* partners *selflessly* giving 100%...not just coughing up a half-baked effort in the hopes that we'll meet in the middle.

Feel free to type this next part out, highlight it, and leave it on your husband's favorite chair. You could also doodle the picture I'm going to attempt to describe below on your bathroom mirror in red lipstick. Visuals help, remember.

Mark Gungor talks in his series, *Laugh Your Way To A Better Marriage*, about the access points to men's and women's hearts. Aptly named, their "*happy* place"[8].

Okay...now put away any persnicketies, dust off your sense of humor and work with me on this, okay?

Imagine two little stick figures, a man and a woman. Bathroom door icons work well here. They each have a heart over their chests, and a smiley face on their privies. Go ahead...sketch it out on a napkin. It's fun.

For a man to touch his wife's, umm...smiley face, he needs to access her **heart** first. Or as Mark succinctly puts it..."*be nice*

91

to the girl!" And as we've discovered already, for us to really access our hubby's hearts...we often need to touch their "happy place" first. Or at least make sure it's getting enough, umm...*happiness*.

Cue the oxytocin, and voila! Call me crazy, but it's worked every time for us!

I've actually doodled this image on dry-erase boards of church fellowship halls across Michigan...only to discover, on occasion, that the marker doesn't always erase completely. Which is just slightly awkward and very funny.

> *"Sex is a balm for their weary souls. Our husbands are out there every day – them against the world – they desperately long for a safe place to come home to, to be completely real and vulnerable, and to be fully accepted and loved. Our desire for them fuels them in a way we will never fully understand"*
>
> *Shaunti Feldhahn*

REFLECTION & ACTION:

- How different is your sex drive, truly, from your husband's? How much of the discrepancy is actually a lack of understanding of how differently we've been wired, or could there be a low-grade simmer of resentment at work?

- Have you noticed the snowball effect of oxytocin in your interest level? When could you initiate an oxytocin dump and get the cycle working in your favor?

- Where has selfishness created a chasm in your intimacy, and what small steps could you take to bridge that gap?

- If the concept of 'the happy place' is new to you, keep your eyes open for it in action, and keep the image in mind as a map for quick heart access (wink wink).

"May your fountain be blessed,
and may you rejoice in the wife of your youth.
A loving doe, a graceful deer –
may her breasts satisfy you always,
may you ever be intoxicated with her love"

Proverbs 5:18-19

10

CHAPTER

HONEY, I HAVE A {LIFE}

Step into this scene with me for a moment, won't you...

The kids are *finally* down and my man walks through the door. It's been a long, hard day for him, but he's finally home in his haven where his guard can drop. Flickers of life return to his batteries, and there stands *his woman*.

His *woah*-man. Can I get a "Halle-*lujah!*"?

Don't misunderstand that as an implication that I look hot.

I don't.

Hot *mess?* Maybe.

I have been home in this 'haven' with these little monsters *all* day. I smell like a science experiment, my hair is pasted down with mashed potatoes on one side and sticking up - compliments of a little person's snot - on the other. It is now only *slightly* longer than my leg hair. My favorite pair of yoga pants, that I've worn for 3 days straight, could probably stand up on their own and will need to be beaten down with a stick to conform to the laundry drum. Which reminds me, the laundry is still piled high on our bed. And those dinner dishes are taunting me from beneath the rubble of the dinner chaos. Ugh.

I have, by this point in the motherhood adventure, come to understand that there is a *massive* chasm between feeling like a *'mum'*, and feeling like a *'woman'*. I do not remotely resemble the latter.

But he cares not. He gives me one of *those* smiles, followed by the *'hey, sexy!'* embrace, strong hands pulling me close.

While I adore his presence and enjoy the attention, I'm very aware of my wall going up. After all, the extent of intelligible conversation I've had all day was about fishy crackers, poop, and the hibernation pattern of brown bears. It was wildly exhilarating, and needless to say, I'm mentally fried. And by this point in the day, my physical affection tank is *beyond* maxed out.

I crave intimacy, really I do. Somewhere deep down in there. It just needs to be beckoned. *Wooed.* I long to be connected with *emotionally* first. Power washed, maybe.

He can practically smell the rubber burning as my mind races through my 'yet-to-do' list, and as my eyes continue to glaze over, he starts to back off. Seeing his spirit deflate, I try reconnecting emotionally but by the time the kettle has boiled, he's fast asleep on the couch, and I'm left lamenting the distance between us.

No, it's *not* romantic, my friend. It's *pathetic*, really. But it's *not uncommon in many marriages today.*

Maybe it's young children. Maybe it's intrusive teenagers. Or maybe it's a tween who never actually made it out of your bed as a wee tyke and nightly positions herself between your bodies as the supportive crossbar in the letter 'H'.

Maybe it's the death of a family member that you never quite got over. Or a job loss that rocked your finances and stole your dream.

Maybe it's menopause. Or a body that has been so drastically changed by pregnancy that you'd wear a wet-suit to bed long before you'd consider lingerie.

Whatever your current reason for not having a dynamic sex life, you're not alone.

It is estimated that one in three married couples struggle with mismatched sexual desire[1].

Newsweek magazine revealed that 15 to 20 percent of married couples have sex no more than 10 times a year[2].

And in a "Mom Confessions" survey done by Family Circle magazine, 32 percent of moms confessed to having gone a few years without having sex[3].

This is *tragic*.

We're facing an epidemic of 'sexless marriages' and it is slowly destroying the family unit. While I'm not naive enough to think that sex is a fix-all for a hurting marriage, because it's most certainly not, we too often underestimate its role in a happy, healthy marriage.

AND THEN THERE WERE THREE

I'll be the first to admit that becoming a mom messes with your sex life on almost every level.

Because while babies may feel like heaven going in...they feel a little more like hell coming out.

Go ahead. Think about it for a minute, you'll get it.

I've heard it said that pregnancy is a 'full body experience' and let me just say, that couldn't be more accurate. Emphasis on *full*. Who knew that growing a human would cause you to snore, drool, pee on yourself, cause certain unmentionables to change color, change the texture of your hair, and increase your shoe size...all at the same time. Sure, I loved the fabulous boobs I acquired in the process, but after a year of nursing each babe, they simply shriveled up, bearing a striking resemblance to deflated balloons.

Skin that once fit me pretty well now sits a little differently, and boasts shiny ribbons that remind me daily that at one point in time, my body was too small to hold more than one human at a time.

I must say, as appalled as you may be by my confession, that one of my favorite things about nursing was discovered quite by accident. My mom and I were sitting in our living room, having a conversation, while I nursed our daughter, Alathea. She was just a few months old and my breasts were still getting acquainted with their new role as a 24-hour milk bar. As my daughter latched on and my milk let down, my hubby walked into the room and distracted her. As she pulled away and turned her head, she got hosed in the face with milk. The hilarity of the moment had my husband hooked and he made a point of distracting her every chance he had. He had no concept of the agony my nipple endured in that head-turning maneuver, so I plotted to get him back.

It wasn't long before the tables were turned. He was sitting across from me one day as the latch-on-let-down routine commenced, and I was ready. He distracted...she turned...and I aimed and *squeezed*! Milk shot across the room with the velocity of a rogue fire hydrant, hitting him square in the kisser. I laughed so hard tears ran down my leg. He was far less amused and that was the end of the nursing distraction.

Just thought you could tuck that little treasure away in your arsenal for future milk wars. You're welcome.

If, like me, you pushed out relatively large babies, chances are your girly parts didn't get off scot free either. And, how shall I say it...? No amount of kegels can undo what those babies did down there. 10 pounds, 6 ounces of delicious baby boy may have come into the world without an ounce of medication, but the hemorrhaging he caused on his way out earned me a front-row seat in surgery. Nubain, a spinal, a cauterized hematoma and stitches later, my southern regions were, well, a wee bit shy.

And then there are the hormones. Oh, my giddy aunt, the *hormones*. I fully intend to talk to God about those when I get to heaven. And I shall be cordial to Eve, despite my urge to throttle her. Rumor has it that's frowned upon in heaven.

SEASONAL (AFFECTION) DISORDER

Creating, birthing and raising humans does a number on your body, if not your sanity, there is *no* doubt about it. And while I love and cherish the experience, I would be foolish to deny that changes have taken place in my marriage.

Denial won't protect us and ignorance is *not* bliss.

Not only do we experience the tangible cycle of seasons each year - in summer we're too hot and sticky to get close for fear we block the limited circulation of air that is keeping us alive, and in Winter we're too stinking cold to want to strip off all those layers and risk hypothermia - every relationship goes through phases and stages. Not only is it natural, but it's necessary for the growth and establishment of the relationship.

Courageously accepting the reality of change provides us the perfect opportunity to tackle challenges as a team, reinforce our commitment, and deepen our connection.

When we stop buying into the lie that society constantly hurls at us, that perfection equals beautiful, and refuse to view our bodies through the lens of superficial hyper-sexuality, we'll learn to love the skin we're in and value the treasure it holds.

Our bodies are an enigma, friend. And while we may never understand them or fully accept their shape, I trust we will learn to appreciate them for the beautiful, miracle-working mysteries they are.

Going from a family of 2 to a family of 3 or more drastically affects your marriage. While it has the potential to enrich, re-fine and bless it tremendously, if you are not prepared for the change, or are unwilling to adapt, you'll miss out on one of the greatest growth opportunities of your entire life. And your relationship will bear the brunt of it.

It amazes me how many women, feeling stuck and lonely in their marriages, wrongly assume adding a child to the mix will fix things. If you thought marriage was hard before, try bring-ing a flesh-sucking, sleep-eradicating, poop machine into your house. It gets all kinds of crazy up in there.

I had no idea I had a temper before I became a mum. Out-bursts of anger never even registered on my radar before these sweet little people interrupted my neatly structured life.

Relative household control was *mine* when it was just me and my man. And then along came our little lady with her flesh-ripping grand entrance, rearranging our lives, calling the shots, and unraveling more than just the toilet paper.

Marriage as we knew it had changed in the blink of a little, pink eyelid. But we still had a choice to make. While, for a season, our children demand more time and attention than our spouse does - after all, they're big enough to feed them-selves and wipe their own bottoms - if we allow our priorities to shift to accommodate that need, without keeping them rooted in the solid foundation of 'God first, spouse second, children third', then when our children eventually grow up and become independent, we're left only with a parenting teammate and not a spouse. Keep your marriage central, and you'll not only model for your kids how to have a happy marriage, you'll protect that relationship for the next season beyond little children.

When we're not prepared for the transition having children has on our relationship, we get stuck mourning a past that will never again be a reality, set ourselves up for failure in the future, and miss the delight of the moment.

DON'T REKINDLE THAT SPARK

I remember when, after graduation, my best friend from high school moved away to college. I stayed home and attended a local community college while getting my feet wet in the wonderful working world. Our lives over the next few years changed so much. While we still had the sweet connection we'd always had, our experience of life as we knew it had been altered completely. There were new people, new lessons, new opportunities, new realities.

I'll never forget the tearful conversation we had when I spent a weekend down at her dorm. I had been lamenting the loss of what had been such an amazing friendship, and even 15 years later, the wisdom and maturity of her response amazes me. She had also been processing the transition of our relationship, but recognized that, in chewing on all the elements involved, we too had changed. It only made sense that our friendship would change.

If we were to desperately attempt to hold on to what we had in high school, we would miss the beauty of the new season we were in. Naturally, there were disappointments and shifts in the roles we would play in each other's lives, and the frequency with which we would see each other, but our willingness to embrace the transition, kept us from missing the new in an effort to cling to the old.

Marriage is in a constant state of motion. Change is inevitable. Trust me, I've tried with all my might to cling to the sweetness of summer when the changes of autumn were imminent.

But here's a profound, if not surprising, truth: *trying to rekindle the spark will get you nowhere.*

Go ahead, read it again. It's a tricky one.

Trying to recreate the connection you experienced at the beginning of your relationship, believe it or not, will do more damage than good.

This is because, attempting to rekindle a gas fire with real wood and matches, not only runs the risk of blowing up in your face, but will hold you back from the *fresh* fire God intends you to build together. For the first 6 to 24 months, your brain is literally dumping a "love drug" into your system. This chemical, phenylethylamine (also referred to as PEA) produces a feeling of euphoria and creates a deep sense of belonging that cannot physically or chemically be recreated in your brain after that time[4].

Gary Thomas talks about the physiology behind the intoxication of a new relationship in his book *Sacred Marriage*[5]. As those feelings start to wear off after the first few years, we realize the full length mirror marriage holds up to us and we rarely like what we see. We recognize the ugliness it brings to the surface and, without the blind love of the newlywed season to cover our inadequacies, we start to drift apart and eventually check out. We then seek a fresh rush of PEA in a new relationship.

The tragedy of this cycle lies in the fact that those chemicals will eventually subside and you'll once again be left with a choice: to press in and press through, or seek the fix of a new infatuation. When we don't stick it out and push through the discomfort, we miss out on the deeper, more satisfying bond that is created over time, and often through adversity.

In the midst of these seasonal shifts, we need to focus on *becoming* a better spouse, rather than *seeking out* a better spouse.

Despite the disappointing lack of PEA in our systems, good news comes in the form of another lovely chemical, oxytocin. As we learned earlier, this 'bonding' chemical is a key player in the nursing mother's 'love-coma' and the after-sex glow, and it dramatically increases as our intimacy increases. While the love drug has come and gone, the bonding agent that connects our hearts and bodies ever deeper, is here to stay. Can I get an "amen"?

KEEPING THE FIRE ALIVE

A year after we moved into our new home, and after 12 months of gasping at propane bills, we decided a wood stove was in order. We did the research, tracked one down in Grand Rapids, hauled the beast home and installed it. Over the past 3 winters of burning wood to heat our home, we've learned a thing or two about trees: all wood is *not* created equal. Some burns hot and fast, leaving us with a heap of ash and a chilly house in the morning. Other wood burns more slowly, but guarantees us a healthy mound of hot embers, ready to be revived, as a new day starts.

We've encountered - and enjoyed - some hot and fast seasons together. But we've found that this type of romance isn't sustainable over the long haul, nor is it realistic. Life has changed drastically since those first years when it was just the two of us, and since those initial neurochemicals stopped throwing those wild parties in our brains. As we've shifted into more of the 'low and slow' burn, we've found that consistency is key in keeping the fire alive.

I remember having one of many discussions with my mom about sex before getting married, and I recall informing her, rather confidently, that we weren't going to have quickies. No, we were going to make passionate love every time. All the time. I had visions of wild naked passion in front of the fireplace, every single night. And then we got married, and life happened, and those wild nights of passion didn't quite pan out the way I had hoped. Something about lack of libido and an abundance of baggage. Not to mention the subsequent loin-fruit that appeared thanks to those occasional nights of passion.

I believe my mom's response to my naiveté that day was a chuckle. A knowing chortle, followed by, *"oh honey, you'll learn to love them!"* And doggone it, that woman was right again.

We happen to have *perfected* the fine art of the quickie over the past few years, which has been incredibly convenient during this season of having little ones.

We love the ability to slip away for a few minutes of fun, especially during the weeks when my husband is working long days (and nights) and has lots of overtime. They're a great way to let off a little steam, release any sexual tension that's built up (primarily for him), and reconnect intimately. But it's not a *sustainable* way to connect. In fact, to avoid the clean-up and enable us to get back into the kitchen before the kids notice we're gone, we usually end up using a condom. We've affectionately come to know these little excursions as taking sex "to go." And I'm sure you can imagine what the 'to-go bag' is.

While these little forays are fun and helpful in busy times, they lack the emotional connection that making love provides.

They're convenient, but *lacking*.

Taking a trip through the drive through for a burger and fries is a convenient way to put some calories in your body without losing much time, but if you adopted this method as your daily eating habit, you'd very quickly find your health decreasing (and your waistline increasing). In the same way this type of diet isn't sustainable or healthy, only having sex or quickies, versus really taking the time to make love to your mate, isn't sustainable or healthy for a marriage.

We need to find a balance between conveniently squeezing each other into our busy schedules, and carving out time for the love of our lives. In short, make sure the majority of your sexual meals are home-cooked, lovingly prepared and slowly enjoyed.

SEX THROUGH THE SEASONS

We cannot manufacture the euphoric giddiness of a new relationship within the boundaries of our marriages, but we can invest in the wealth of connection that will propel us into a sweeter, more intimate future together. The wisdom, maturity and resilience we've gained in the past decade is far more valuable than a sky-high libido and sweaty palms.

There are perpetual transitions in marriage, and the more we embrace this truth, the more resilient and unyielding our marriage becomes throughout those changes.

While these distinct seasons can massively impact the frequency and expression of sexual fulfillment, if we don't intentionally work to bring it back to the forefront - in whatever unique expression best fits that season - we will lose ground in our marriages.

I recall, when our oldest was 3 and didn't have a clue how to read, we'd hijack the kid's bath crayons and write naughty messages to each other on our shower wall. While doodles and pictograms had to be kept to a minimum, we had complete freedom in the verbiage department. Then came the day - rather suddenly, it seemed - that she started sounding things out.

"Mommy...why does it say, "I...like...you...uh, your...pen...pen... pen is...on the shower wall? And what is a pen-is, Mommy?"

Seasons.

Now we get to find other creative ways to play, and flirtatiously hint at the possibility of a rendezvous in the near future without involving words located in easily readable locations.

While I can't personally speak to the time frame of marriage beyond what we know, I do believe the principles and practices - while dynamic - remain the same. I am beyond blessed to have a mom and dad who are deeply committed to each other and still giggle about the romp they enjoyed before breakfast. They did an amazing job of raising us four girls, but always made it clear that their marriage came first. We may not have understood or appreciated their dedication then, but we treasure it now. By preserving and prioritizing their marriage while we were little, they protected it for the future. Rather than awkwardly looking at each other once the youngest had moved out, wondering what on earth had happened to their relationship, they reveled in their newfound ability to once again rule the roost. Naked. With almost 40 years of marriage under their belts, they've fleshed out a stunning example of a marriage after God's own heart.

Cultivating a sex life that withstands the test of time, and not only survives, but thrives, through the many seasons of life, demands *creativity, flexibility and determination*.

When we allow the busyness of life to suck us dry, we set ourselves up for marital disaster. A great marriage has *got* to have *emotional, spiritual and physical* connectedness at its core. When even one of those elements is suffering, they all suffer.

"Sex is the spice that rescues our relationships from becoming mundane pursuits of chores" Bill & Pam Farrell[6].

GETTING IT RIGHT

If you had a fractured bone that caused pain and discomfort every time you put pressure on it, you would find a way to deal with the pain. Medicating it only works for so long. In fact, the longer you numb it and walk on it, gritting your teeth and braving the pain, the more damage you'll do in the long run. Something this major requires the expertise of a surgeon, the precision of a scalpel and the power of steel to repair and mend what is broken.

And to remove what is causing the interference.

I learned a brilliant equation during my life coach training earlier this year: **P = p – i** [7]

Our *performance (P)* is equal to our *potential (p)* minus *interference (i)*. While marriage isn't about performance, per se, our ability to perform our role as a wife - the fully alive, healthy woman who stands strong beside her man - is crippled by 'interference'. That interference may look very different for you than it does for me, or your sister, or your best girlfriend. The fact remains, it hinders your potential as long as it is allowed to remain in the marriage equation.

We would be foolish to avoid a medical surgery simply because it would cause further - albeit temporary - discomfort, and inconvenience, and would be accompanied by a period of intense recovery.

Thankfully, when it comes to our marriages, we have a Master Surgeon whose specialty is identifying and removing the interference or infection, dealing with the fracture, healing the broken[hearted], and restoring the connection.

But here's the thing about this Surgeon; we have to make ourselves available to Him. He's a gentleman like that.

Wooing is done *without* your permission. Reconstructive surgery is not.

Want a marriage that's solid, whether basking in the warmth of a summer sweet-spot, or enduring the chill of a winter freeze? Whether indulging in the multi-layered cake of the newlywed experience, or inching your way through the well-seasoned stages of old age together?

Learn from the past, press into your present, and invite the Surgeon into your future.

Appreciate the old, embrace the new, and always - always - *choose joy in the moment.*

REFLECTION & ACTION:

- What season do you feel you are in right now? Would your husband agree with that assessment?

- What are your favorite characteristics of the season of life you're currently in as a couple? What are the hardest parts?

- In what creative way could you foster a spirit of fun and freedom in your sexual intimacy during this season?

- Search out an older couple who have a decade or more marital experience than you, who have a healthy, vibrant connection (and are maybe enjoying the freedom of the empty nest season). Walk alongside them, watch, listen and learn from them. Then, come alongside a younger couple who are a few years behind you in marriage, who are maybe in a tougher season (in the trenches of tod-dlerdom or wrestling with infertility) and be a source of life and encouragement to *them*. This biblical posture of one hand forward (learning) and one hand back (leading) links our hearts to couples in other seasons, equips us with unique relational tools, and broadens our life experience.

"He has made everything beautiful in its time"

Ecclesiastes 3:11a

11

CHAPTER

STOP, DROP AND ROLL

We got a delightful taste of 'community living' when, after 11 months spent in their house while my husband was laid off, my parents moved onto our property. It wasn't long into their almost two years with us before they'd changed the "man cave" into the "love shack." No explanation is really needed on this one.

They had moved up from their home, which was an hour directly South of us and was being rented out at the time, because the city they had started a church in, and where my dad taught at the local college, was considerably closer to *us* than to *them*. We were thrilled to be able to offer them the 600 square foot semi-finished half of the man cave as their own, separated from the garage side by a metal door.

This building, which was the first structure built on our property 15 years ago by the original owners, functioned as their bare-bones living space while they built the main house. The moment we laid eyes on it we had grand plans to turn it into a little guest house, and with the sudden absorption of my parents into our daily life, it quickly became what we call in Southern Africa, a "granny flat."

Apart from the lack of conventional heat or air conditioning, the unattractive cement floor, and the fact that the shower feels like you're standing under a dripping faucet - or better yet, a drooling child - it was a comfortable studio apartment. Boasting double french doors that overlook the neighboring pond, a minimalist kitchen corner, and a little bathroom, it's a lovely little space.

Whenever my mom had time during the day, she'd load up her toiletries, towel and clothes, and head across the yard into our house for a *proper* shower. One that actually involved more than 5 drops of water emerging from the shower head at one time, and one with considerably more velocity than their syrup dripper.

When they moved out last summer and found a space of their own in the community they longed to call home, they were thrilled to unpack all the things they'd had in storage for two years...but then were disappointed to discover that, yet again, they had landed in a home without any sort of substantial water pressure.

So as it turns out, whenever we have a date night and my parents come over to watch the kids, mom brings her toiletry bag and washcloth. Because this woman is going to get a quality shower if it kills her. I admire her dedication to power-washed hygiene.

The funny thing is, I didn't even *know* our shower was that awesome. Well, I suppose I did when we *first* moved in. I recall loving how different it was from our previous, dribbly shower. But then, as with all good things, we soon became accustomed to it and grow to *expect* it. Sure, a mission trip would instill some good old fashioned hot-water-treasuring gratitude in me, but it usually takes seeing my mom walk into the house, toiletry bag in hand, to remember that we have a pretty kickin' shower.

I'm like this with a lot of things in life, sadly, including my marriage. And if I were to hazard a guess, I'd say you probably are too, to some extent.

My husband happens to kick butt. Literally, if the bad guys run from him, and figuratively. Before we met, after coming out of a slew of miserable, destructive relationships - if one could call them that - I was encouraged to put together a list of characteristics I would commit to pray for in a husband. I had scribbled a list on my teenage heart several years prior, and simply lopped off the unmet qualifiers when a semi-eligible dude showed up. Nah, he doesn't need to be sporty. Or polite. Or a Christian...really, those things can all happen over time. But tall? He has got to be tall. And off I'd go, happily cutting and pasting items from my mental list to justify the hopeless fling of the week.

But this time, after having been celibate for 3 years, I got serious. I wrote down all the things I felt were non-negotiables in a husband, and in the future father of our children. I committed to not settle for "an eyelash less" than who God had for me.

Integrity, I jotted down, *tender hearted, funny, strong leader...passionate about Jesus, tall*, of course...*ambitious, adventurous, fiercely loyal*. And on it went. It felt silly at times, but I'd allowed myself to compromise on the big things long enough to realize that certain things couldn't afford to be left off, and I had to know what I was looking for or else I'd settle for less. And when I say "looking for," I don't mean that I prowled around town, peering under church pews for the most eligible bachelor. I had been challenged by a mentor to stop looking and to focus on my relationship with God, allowing Him time to heal my heart and room to restore my identity as I waited on His perfect timing.

But I needed to know what to look for, and what to avoid, when someone did cross my path.

When Joe and I met, we were both 21 and he was in a pretty serious relationship. Despite our inability to catch onto the fact that we kept running into each other for a reason, living over an hour away from each other, he just happened to be everything on my list and then some. He even had large hands, loved to break out in song at random times, and regularly smelled scrumptious...petty things I'd considered writing down before I realized just how ridiculous they were to request in a spouse. They were just freebies from a God who knew my heart even better than I did.

But skip forward a few years and, in the crux of young parenthood, do you think I cared that he was all those fabulous things and more? No. Heck no. All I cared about was that he kept leaving his freaking socks on the floor in the bathroom, his clothes next to the bed, his coffee cup next to the couch, and his perfect manners at work.

Isn't it astounding how quickly our focus can shift from how fantastic someone is, with all their strengths and fabulous character traits, to what a moron they can be, with all their weaknesses and inadequacies?

Sheesh, if only they'd stop being so human.

It is amazing how easily we take things for granted once we've experienced them for a period of time. Remember thinking, *"just wait until I...(fill in whatever goal, position or achievement you were working toward at one time or another),"* and then once you achieved it, you were onto bigger and better things.

We want something if we don't have it, but once we get it, and get used to it, we want *more.* Or something else entirely.

It's the fatal flaw of humanity. It's what tripped Eve up in the garden. There they were, just chilling in the original paradise, naked as newborns. They had everything at their fingertips, including a palpable intimacy with their Father God, but Eve wanted the one thing she couldn't have. She bought the lie we all buy at some point: *that God is holding out on us.*

We believe that if we are to be happy and content, we've got to take matters into our own hands and go after something we think we don't yet have. But in the end, "it" isn't what satisfies us at all, and we find that we've wished away what we did have.

The sooner we can learn to catch ourselves in this downward spiral of discontentment, we can retrain our hearts to focus on all we *do* have and cultivate an attitude of gratitude in our homes.

As we've heard it said, *gratitude turns what we have into enough,* and how true that has turned out to be. Especially within the melting pot of the marriage covenant.

STOP TRYING TO CHANGE HIM

As if the polar opposites of male and female brains and bodies weren't paradoxical enough, throw in a hefty helping of family history, a sprinkling of temperament, personality differences and birth-order influence, a truckload of strengths, weaknesses, unique skills and interests, along with a few spoonfuls of love languages that you probably don't speak naturally...and you've got yourself a potential disaster just waiting to happen. If you're really lucky, you'll have some cultural differences to contend with too. This appears to be reserved for extra special folk who apparently need additional refining.

It's a miracle, really, that any marriage survives, all things considered. This divine conspiracy conjured up in the heart of God, that requires His daily input to survive, is a mystery. And few of us realized this coming into it.

Maybe our naiveté is *required* in order for us to board the ship. Marriage is most certainly the ride of our lives and I wonder whether, if we knew just how intensely we'd be stretched and challenged, we would actually have stepped out and grabbed on.

As we've worked through some of our more substantial differences, much like the physical ones we've already talked about, we're learning to embrace and celebrate them, rather than wrestle with and resent them.

It's easy to want to make ourselves feel better about the choices we make and the way we naturally respond to things by getting black-and-white about things that were never intended to be black-and-white.

New moms face this as they navigate the unchartered waters of young motherhood. Natural delivery or epidural. To vaccinate or not. Breast or bottle. Stay at home or return to work. Home-school or public. And on it goes. In an effort to lessen the insecurity we feel about our own decisions, we passionately claim our way is the right way, and promptly label those on the opposite side of the fence as wrong.

I'm thankful my exit from the mommy mafia occurred sooner than later, and is partly due to a mantra we adopted early on in marriage: *it's not wrong, it's just different*.

And sure, while some things are obviously wrong, many things we tend to label as wrong are in fact just wrong for *us*.

One of the paradigm shifts we experienced within the first few years of marriage was discovered through Emerson Eggerichs' *Love & Respect* series[1]. There were big bulbs lighting up for us here.

Emerson presents the theory that respect is like oxygen to men. When someone shows disrespect to a man, they're essentially stepping on his "air hose." And likewise, love is like oxygen to women. When deprived of this life-source, we lash out in an effort to regain our oxygen, which often comes across as disrespectful or unloving.

This initiates what he refers to as the 'crazy cycle'.

We communicate in a way that is interpreted as disrespectful to our men, and they react in a way that feels unloving to us, so we hit them where it hurts - again - and on the cycle goes. He goes on to explain that it's not that men don't need love, and women don't need respect, it's simply that our native tongues come naturally to us. Women don't typically need to be told to love, and men don't typically need to be encouraged to show respect. It's a currency we deal in. Of course, there are always those who don't fit into the general 'stereotype', but in most cases, this information inspires a lot of 'ah-ha' moments in marriages.

In a national survey done by Shaunti Feldhahn, she asked men and women whether they'd rather feel alone and unloved, or inadequate and disrespected. As I'm sure you've already guessed, the majority of women said they'd rather feel "inadequate and disrespected," while the men indicated that "alone and unloved" was by far less painful than the alternative[2].

Don't try to rationalize and understand this concept. It really doesn't make much sense to us because we are wired so differently. But don't let your lack of comprehension keep you from intentionally honoring that desire in your man.

The good news, as Emerson expanded on in the Love & Respect series, is that there is also an energizing cycle. While the crazy cycle is set into motion by the lack of expressed love or respect, the energizing cycle is triggered by someone choosing to meet that need for respect or love, whether it's 'deserved' or not, and this inspires from the other, another act of love or respect, and off it goes.

We've seen both of these cycles in action multiple times over the course of the past several years, and being able to identify them has actually made it more fun to call it out. There's something to be said about being able to recognize the face of your enemy, and sometimes the simple lack of love and respect in our interaction is the culprit.

We've also been known to throw out lines like, *"you're stepping on my air-hose, dude!"* which quickly points to the problem and exposes the need for one of us to step up and initiate the energizing cycle.

DROP THE WEAPON

Have you ever noticed how we can be kind, courteous, and respectful to friends – or even complete strangers – then turn around and be quite the opposite to the very one we committed to love and cherish? It's pretty sad, really.

As essential as our outer presentation is, which we talked about in the previous chapter, our inner presentation is *far more* critical to the emotional well-being of our marriage.

Making room in your marriage for great sex is less about how you position your pelvis and more about how you position your heart.

The Bible says that the power of life and death are in the tongue[3]. That's one powerful little muscle we flap around in our skull caves, often without much thought to the effect it has on others.

We need to ask ourselves, when we're tempted to run at the mouth, whether we are speaking *life,* or *death,* to our husbands, and over our marriages.

In a world that daily informs us where we fall short, and constantly chips away at our self-esteem by reminding us of what we're not, we need to be reminding each other of who we *are*. We need to be the voice of truth to our spouse, not a feeder of lies. It is so important that we learn to speak destiny and purpose over each other.

Just like our external presentation, after a few years of marriage, our *heart* presentation, or attitude, can slip if we're not careful. The once easy laughter and encouragement may become cold retorts and nagging.

Ever wondered what happened to the fun and flirting and *resilience* you once enjoyed as friends?

A danger that creeps in here is the tendency to be more thoughtful and helpful to coworkers and friends, because of the lavish thanks and praise it elicits, while dropping the ball on our spouse. We may not receive the same response, but it doesn't negate our responsibility to serve and assist.

On the other end of the spectrum, we can see why sometimes serving around the house doesn't bring them the joy it does when serving elsewhere. In zeroing in on all the things that have *yet* to get done in our busy lives, it is easy to take our spouse's small acts of kindness for granted. When my hubby loads the dishwasher and puts away food after a meal, it's not unusual for me to walk back into the kitchen later on and, rather than enthusiastically thanking him for what he *has* done, I'll casually point out the mess on the counters, then simply get to work wiping and scrubbing. I don't intentionally negate the effort he's made, but by focusing on the little things he *didn't* do rather than thanking him for what he *did* do, I do just that.

The moment we stop being thankful and we start nagging and nitpicking, we've sucked the joy and life out of our friendship. I don't know about you, but I don't tend to enjoy – or intentionally plan - to be around people who drain the life from the room.

We have got to fight for our *friendship* within our marriage. It's a crucial color in this brilliant work of art. We need to be intentional about smiling at our hubbies when they walk into a room, rather than unloading our concerns and needs.

Let's once again laugh at their silly jokes, and ridiculous bodily functions. And, my goodness, let's stop being *so serious and easily offended.*

We need to learn how to flirt again. Go ahead...pinch those meaty cheeks!

LEARN TO FIGHT RIGHT

Because we were created so very differently, it is *inevitable* that conflict will arise. It isn't *whether* we disagree; it's all about *how* we do it. While we've never had a knock-down, drag-out fight, nor are we shouters, we do deal with our fair share of what we've affectionately come to know as "*intense fellowship.*"

It's so important that we realize that we accomplish nothing when we battle against each other, when the real enemy isn't even flesh and blood (Ephesians 6:12). In fact, we do the devil's work for him when we cut each other down rather than build each other up.

So, what *do* we do when we're hurt, offended, or just royally ticked off about something?

First, we need to step back and evaluate the big picture.

As someone who's spent many years parenting alone in the evening hours, while my husband was at work, I've had many late night phone conversations that sounded somewhat like this: "*How was your day, babe? How were the kids?*" he'd ask.

(Insert a long pause and dramatic sigh for effect) "*Ugh! Long and frustrating. I am not cut out for this parenting gig. How do single mothers do it? The kids were complete monsters to-day...at each other's throats constantly, not listening or being obedient...I think I've pulled half of my hair out already. Put-*

ting them on the curb with a 'buy one, get one free' sign taped to their heads sounded like a fabulous plan an hour ago!"

I promise, I was an excellent mother before I had children. Now I'm just excellent client material for therapists. Go figure.

As I'd sit, tea in hand, the next morning - distanced from the events of the day before by a decent night's rest and some physical separation, my heart would ache. I so over-reacted. When asked what exactly the kids did to render it such a pitiful night, my description of the offenses would never sound as dreadful as they'd felt in the moment. I'd realize, in being able to process through their actions and my subsequent *reactions*, that I was just as much to blame for the misery. On any "normal" day, my world would not have been so rocked by their antics.

I am a very task-oriented person, and when my head is wrapped up in a project or in preparation for something, I tend to see my children as a distraction, or an annoyance, rather than the priority they are.

My visceral response to their childish behavior was a result of my desire to get done what *I* wanted to get done. And as I continue to reflect on what was really going on during my "awful day," it's clear that most of the mess was my responsibility, and unless I own it, it won't get resolved.

I think we do this to our hubbies a lot. We sabotage them when our perception of a situation is based solely on the lens through which we look, and rarely is it an entirely unselfish one.

So the first step in learning how to 'fight right', is *owning your part*. Being able to dissect a situation from a more unbiased perspective and claim the role you've played. I've found it to be immensely helpful to ask God to help me with this process. I'll simply ask, "*Lord, show me where I'm placing my issues on him, and reveal what the real issue is so that we can tackle the root without getting caught up in the branches."*

This also acts as an excellent diffuser of unnecessary anger or frustration.

Next, it's important to deal with the situation as soon as humanly possible.

We made a commitment, before we even got married, to never let the sun go down on our anger (Ephesians 4:26). While I tend to be a stewer, and want to nurse my wounds for a while, my husband ruins this every time. He will pursue me and graciously get in my face until we've worked it out. While it's wildly frustrating in the moment, I am so very thankful for his persistence and his honoring of our commitment.

The longer we allow stuff to sit and fester, the greater the opportunity for misunderstanding, bitterness and resentment. We also open ourselves up to temptation and greater attack by giving the enemy a foothold in our marriage.

At the same time, it is so important not to run our mouths to friends or other family members about our frustration. Our husbands operate on a respect system that is seriously violated when we talk to others *about* them, rather than going directly *to* them. While it's good to have someone we can talk to about our marital struggles who will offer wise counsel (a mom, a mentor, a best friend, etc.), we need to be certain that this person loves, respects and honors our husband. If they don't, they won't help diffuse our frustration, they'll simply add to it.

Everyone brings something to the fire of personal conflict. Align yourself with people who bring water, rather than those who pour fuel.

Choose your words wisely.

Once those piercing accusations have left your lips, you cannot take them back. Think carefully through your words before you deliver them. Rather than character assassination or ruthless accusation, which simply send their walls shooting up, share your concerns by saying, *"I feel as though you don't..."* or *"My heart feels trampled every time you..."* The moment we start with, *"You never meet my needs..."* or *"You always make me feel this way,"* we've lost them.

It's incredibly important to avoid getting all historical on them. If there are issues from months, or years, ago that you haven't dealt with, don't allow them to flavor the conversation *today*. Deal with the problem at hand, and when you're not ready to throttle each other, try to identify the root issues you might still need to tackle.

If something happened a while back that *has* been dealt with, don't bring it back up again. It is unfair to resuscitate past offenses that you've forgiven them for. If it's over, put it to rest.

Sometimes correcting our approach to an issue is simply a matter of us choosing not to be so easily offended, and to be a little more resilient and forgiving.

Some of the best phrases you can learn in marriage come in threes: *"I was wrong," "I am sorry"* and *"Please forgive me."*

Always choose unity.

Above all, remember that unity is far more important than the cheap thrill of being right. We are called to lay down our lives for each other, to be slow to speak and slow to anger[4], to be quick to listen and quick to forgive[5], and to not keep a record of wrongs[6].

Whew. It seems like an impossibly high standard to live by, but it's one we're called to pursue and embrace, and it's the very language of grace that won our affection and saved our souls in the first place.

There's no better place to practice this extravagant love than in our own marriages.

> *"But God demonstrates his own love for us in this:*
> *While we were still sinners, Christ died for us"*
>
> Romans 5:8

ROLL WITH THEIR FLUENCY

Another enormously useful tool in our marital tool belt has been exploring our unique love languages. In the fantastic book, *The Five Love Languages*, Gary Chapman writes about the importance of identifying and expressing love to your spouse in a way that he (or she) can understand[7].

It's all fine and dandy speaking Spanish to your guy when that's his native tongue, but if he's Afrikaans, you better learn how to *"praat die taal"*[8] if you ever hope to communicate in a way he'll understand.

And so it is with what he coins *'the five love languages'*.

They are: acts of service, quality time, words of affirmation, gifts and physical touch.

I firmly believe that we all need all five to some degree, but we do tend to express and receive love primarily through two or three of these languages. An interesting thing I've noticed over the years, since first learning about this book, is that my primary love languages changed over time.

While *physical touch* used to be a biggie for me years ago, since becoming a mom, my physical touch tank is usually pretty maxed out. *Acts of service* has conveniently leapt to the top of the list. Wash my dishes and clean the kitchen floor and, woah baby, am I feeling the love. My hubby often fills up my gas tank and refills my tea cup - not because I can't - but because he knows it blesses me when he does.

Words of affirmation is my other native tongue. While I speak it naturally, and feel *über* loved when others encourage and affirm me, I can tell my hubby how awesome he is until I'm blue in the face, but if I'm not spending quality time with him, hearing his heart and genuinely sharing mine with him, his love tank will remain unfilled. Because that isn't his primary love language. He's a *quality time* and *physical touch* kind of guy. Go figure.

How do you express love? Are you a gift giver? Do you see little things at the store that make you think of others, so you pick it up for them just to let them know you were thinking about them?

You see, this whole love language thing isn't just about marriage. It's how we communicate and receive love across the board. In fact, Gary Chapman has since come out with a book specifically geared towards kids, *The Five Love Languages of Children*.

I would encourage you to read the original book for a better understanding of the five languages, and then start examining how you and your spouse communicate love. It's easy to stew quietly when we feel our love tanks are running on empty...but we need to remember that our primary language of love may not come naturally to our spouse. Here's where communication is key! While some expressions of love may come effortlessly to us, it is so worth it for us to become fluent in their primary love languages, and they in ours.

It has been hard for me to prioritize quality time with my hubby. It may sound ridiculous to admit, but while I love spending time with him, being the chronic multitasking busy-body that I am, I'm totally happy for us to be doing multiple things at the same time. I love our long, uninterrupted heart-to-hearts, but he needs them more frequently than I do. He craves eye-contact and proximity to a greater extent than I do. He loves it when he's working on a project out in the garage and I come out and just hang with him. But it darn near kills me. There is always so much I could be doing elsewhere, so much vying for my attention, and to silence those urges and just be present with him takes sacrifice. I often want to do what I want to do, but marriage is a lesson in dying to self.

When I go out of my way to speak love through these avenues, his tank overflows and he's more apt to seek ways to communicate love in the languages that speak most profoundly to *my* heart.

And then, when both our love tanks are brimming, sexual intimacy happens naturally in the overflow of that closeness. When we allow our tanks to run dry, and become frustrated by the lack of response to the (love) language we speak so easily, initiating intimacy suddenly feels awkward and contrived.

This is revelatory stuff and has the potential to completely transform your ability to communicate more intimately with your spouse. Think of this material as the long lost translator between two alien planets.

Help is on the way, friend. *Mweep mweep.*

In all seriousness, we have a choice to make. We can choose to speak life to our precious men, or we can speak death. Our words are unbelievably powerful.

As women, we are influential beyond what we comprehend. It's in our DNA. We set the tone and atmosphere of our homes, while creating the lens through which our children will see their daddy. When we speak ill of our men, we tarnish our children's view, and hamper their ability to see the good in their daddies.

While praise is conditional, and tends to focus on accomplishment or competency, encouragement and validation are unconditional, and coincidentally, always in style. So dish it out, sister!

When our husbands feel championed by their wives, the hero in them rises to the surface.

God intends for us to be passionate gold diggers[9]. Relentlessly unearthing the treasure in others. He has deposited greatness in every single one of us, and we have the opportunity, no...the awesome *responsibility*, as wives, to help mine that treasure and bring the greatness in our husbands, to the surface.

REFLECTION & ACTION:

- What are some of the qualities and characteristics that first attracted you to your husband?

- What about your husband have you grown so accustomed to that it's easy to take for granted? What would it look like for you to re-cultivate an attitude of gratitude in these areas?

- Where have you placed expectations on your husband to behave or process things like you do? How might releasing them to be different, enhance your relationship?

- With a greater understanding of your need for love, and his need for respect, be on the lookout for signs that you might be stepping on each other's air-hose (for example, a sudden withdrawal, or a 'deflated' spirit).

- What are your top two love languages? What are your husband's? Acts of service, words of affirmation, gifts, physical touch or quality time? In what way could you practice speaking his native tongue this week?

- How do you tend to handle conflict, and what checks and balances could you put in place to handle it more effectively in the future?

- Ask God to place a guard over your heart and a filter in your mouth. Choose to speak more love, grace and encouragement rather than criticism and complaint.

"An unfriendly person pursues selfish ends
and against all sound judgment starts quarrels.
Fools find no pleasure in understanding
but delight in airing their own opinions"

Proverbs 18:1-2

12

CHAPTER

THE JOY THIEF

While the temptation to compare myself to others - most often my weaknesses to their strengths, or my behind-the-scenes blooper reel to their polished highlights reel - is still very much a struggle for me, I am very selective about what I allow to steal my joy. I've fought long and hard to reclaim it. But there are days I will give it away, without so much as a fight, to a sleep-deprived, grumpy hubby.

Communication didn't appear to be something we would struggle with in the beginning, but then again, what really *does* when you're doe-eyed and hormonally hyped-up?

We connected effortlessly in conversation, laughing about silly things and providing the token shoulder when things got deep and uncomfortable. We would talk for hours about the dreams and hopes we had percolating inside us, and for the first few years, 'effort' and 'intentionality' weren't really necessary. Communication just happened.

But then our little ones came along, smoking cigars and calling the shots, occupations changed, responsibilities increased, and opportunities to connect became less frequent. The less often we talked about deep, heart stuff, the harder it became to initiate those conversations. Eventually you get so comfortable functioning like ships passing in the night, you almost forget what you're missing out on, and before you know it, you feel like strangers sleeping in the same bed.

And if the thought of sex with a stranger was remotely interesting before, it's not with this one. It's incredibly hard to want to be intimate with someone you feel you no longer know, and who doesn't know you.

Everything sweet and intimate slowly fizzles out until you're left feeling completely alone in your marriage, trying to figure out how on earth you're going to live like this for the rest of your life.

Good communication is foundational in a successful marriage. When couples stop talking about the stuff that really matters, it's no wonder they feel as if the ground is crumbling beneath them. They're left without anything substantial to build their future on.

My hubby and I really struggled with this during his first few years in law enforcement. He would come home from his shift, tired and yet with adrenaline still coursing through his system. Still freshly indoctrinated with the cockiness of having worked hard for that badge, he would move around the house with the same authoritative distance that keeps him alive on the road. His brow seemed permanently molded into a frown, and he startled easily when life happened loudly, which in a house with two little children, was every 7.3 seconds.

Tenderness and grace seemed like qualities he'd somewhat lost touch with.

The moment I would notice my spirit deflating simply by being in the same room as him, I would try to subtly avoid him. I would occasionally mumble comments in passing about him having failed to take off his uniform yet, or better yet, the "*I'm your WIFE...not a criminal!*" comment when common courtesies were forgotten.

Those were some long, hard years for our marriage. While he processed the weight of his career choice, daily risking his life to defend and protect people, many of whom have no respect for his profession, I was silently mourning the loss of my tender-hearted, fun-loving best friend. The tension was thick.

While many admired my strength and courage, in light of my husband's occupation, it was merely the pretty wrapping around a deeply fearful heart. I was terrified that I would lose him - not physically, but emotionally - to the cynicism and negativity that runs rampant in the law enforcement world. The heart callous functions like the Kevlar on their chests. And so the defenses they set up to keep the bad out end up keeping the good out too, as they try desperately to numb the pain of constantly fighting on the front lines of a depraved and broken world.

It's no wonder many law enforcement marriages don't survive.

After a particularly awkward dance of avoidance, that had spanned a few days, he cornered me in the laundry room.

"*What's wrong, babe?*"

"*Nothing,*" I spat out, trying to get past him.

And here that whole 'bigger and stronger and taller' petition came back to bite me in the butt. He stood square in the doorway and wouldn't let me through.

"*Why won't you even look me in the eyes?*" he pressed.

And the floodgates opened. Three years of frustration and fear came gushing out and hit him square between the eyes.

"*Because you're a jerk! You are so rude to me for no reason at all...instead of asking me nicely to move, you body-slam me out of your way as if I'm some kind of felon. You are so full of yourself that you can't fathom the possibility that you might actually be wrong about something. Why are you so unkind to my parents? Your tiredness and inability to function on our schedule doesn't excuse your behavior! And sex? Why the hell would I want to be intimate with someone I don't even feel like I know anymore. You...are...not...safe for my heart anymore! Because you're being an ASS!*"

Voice cracking, tears streaming, I squeezed past him and sought refuge in our bathroom.

But, being the man he is, he pursued me. Not to fight. But to make right what he had so clearly allowed to go wrong.

This was one of the few monumental eruptions I've experienced over the course of our marriage. I'm not a yeller or a screamer when it comes to my husband. I'm not really a fighter. Not that this is entirely a good thing. I tend to be passive aggressive about things that bother me, and rather than risk rocking the boat by dealing with them head on, I just stuff them away and pretend they don't bother me. But they do. Despite the smile and happiness I may earnestly exude on the outside, those wounds grow and fester, and when I least expect it, they explode.

And it's never pretty. But it's always good.

"*I need you to call me out on this, love. That's one of your roles as my wife...to hold me accountable, and when I'm slipping up and not treating you the way I should...don't just take it. Please. I'm giving you permission to call me on the carpet. I NEED you to do this. If not for you, for me. This matters to me and you need to speak up.*"

It felt so good to communicate again. Even if it was inconvenient and unpleasant at the time. It was real and raw and honest and ugly. But it gave birth to a beautiful thing: a freshly prioritized transparency that the health of our marriage depended on.

BREATHE INTO IT

We've had this conversation a few times since that cleansing day in the laundry room, only with less heat and venom. You see, we laid a foundation and created a safe place for this subject to be discussed, so when it does rear its ugly head, we're able to deal with it so much faster.

A vibrant marriage requires our naked-heart contribution. Without our voices to bring insight and clarity, we suffer in silence and slowly grow apart.

I cannot tell you how many times I've found myself crouched down in front of the wood stove in the middle of winter, trying desperately to bring it back to life. My husband would load it before he'd leave for work in the early afternoon and it would be good to go for hours. But then I'd get busy with work and home and munchkins returning from school and, still basking in the afterglow of its radiant heat, would completely forget to reload it. Suddenly a chill in the air would grab my attention. There, in the woodstove, mocking me, would be a mound of ash.

I'm no Bear Grylls, but I've discovered a thing or two about starting - and rekindling - fires over the past few years of heating with wood. I've learned that springing into action at even the slightest signs of life in those embers can save a fire. Strategically building my tower with small pieces of wood, I'd stuff it with crumpled paper and blow. Quickly catching, the paper would burst into flame and the fire would roar. For a minute. Just as the paper would start to die down, I'd fill my lungs and blow. Long and hard. Blowing on it, in the moment, would seem so counterproductive because the flame would almost completely die back and appear to fizzle out, but the nanosecond my lungs where emptied, it would burst back into flame, bigger and hotter than before.

I find this to be true in the outpouring and rekindling of communication in my marriage. If I'm attentive to the embers and am intentional about breathing life into them the moment I recognize a temperature change, we can quickly restore what has been lost. The dilemma occurs when I am breathing out my heart, vulnerably and honestly, and worrying how it might be received. I instantly want to pull it all back in for fear that it extinguish the flame. It's easy, in those moments, to want to retreat and simply stuff my emotions, but if I'm gracious and wise in my timing, ever bringing oxygen to the fire of our relationship, it gets stronger and hotter every time.

NON-VERBAL

Communication runs so much deeper than just words. In fact I've heard that almost 90 percent of communication is non-verbal[1]. What we don't say, can say so much. Our facial expressions, body language and even muscle rigidity communicate more than we realize.

For women who tend to talk less about their concerns and choose rather to stuff their frustration, body language is particularly powerful. It's as though the negativity that gets crammed down deep leaks from our pores and speaks volumes without saying a word.

Another layer of the proverbial onion that God peeled back during the first few years of married life was my default response to emotionally disconnect while remaining physically present during intimacy. You'd have thought rigor mortis was beginning to set in.

I had developed this response as a young teenager as a way of escaping the war that raged within my heart. I hated the cycle of promiscuity I was caught up in, and the filth I felt utterly stuck in, but I couldn't seem to get out, so I simply disengaged.

I didn't identify this as being the root of my response for the first few years of marriage, so my poor hubby was left to feel that his wife wasn't even interested in being there in the moment with him. Without ever intending to, I had communicated my dislike of sex, my desire to be elsewhere, and my lack of interest in him.

Learning to re-engage during intimacy took time, courage and prayer. While it's still easy to get distracted and sucked into the swirling vortex of to-do lists and schedules, choosing to be present, emotionally, with my man is the only way to protect that bond and cultivate the closeness and security we crave in our marriage.

Good communication isn't optional in a great marriage, it's a necessity that we have to make a conscious effort to prioritize. Along with discussing the big, important moments in our lives, creating space to connect daily about the seemingly less significant things is essential.

As any parent with small children knows, this is considerably easier said than done. While we'll occasionally encourage them to go and spend a little time in the family room, so that we can actually finish a sentence, we also try to connect over a cup of coffee or tea while they're playing around us. It's important for them to see us making time for each other, prioritizing our marriage, while giving them the opportunity to practice the lost art of not interrupting us every 32 seconds. It's a win-win situation.

Along with verbalizing our affection and love for each other frequently throughout the day, be it in person or via a text or call, we try and schedule regular date nights where we can break routine and enjoy each other's company and conversation. We like to dream when we go on dates. We talk about what's stirring in our hearts, what gets us excited, and what we're dreaming up for the future. We intentionally try *not* to spend the entire time talking about the kids or what's going on at work.

While we may not always be on the same page, or agree with everything the other one says, there's a blanket understanding that our marriage is a safe place to be real and vulnerable, and we work hard to keep it that way. No topic or struggle is unwelcome at the table.

JUST PLAY

It's so important to find something you enjoy doing together, be it going to the movies, golfing, fishing, or simply going for walks. Finding a hobby you can share helps protect your friendship, and unites your hearts during some of the most stressful years of marriage. We have discovered a mutual love for canoeing and road trips, a shared affection for Jack Bauer of 24, and trying new ethnic restaurants.

Having fun together is one of the fastest and most effective ways to take your marriage from 'blah' to 'hoorah!'.

Sometime last year, after a late brunch of chocolate pancakes and fresh fruit, we were cleaning up the kitchen when I got hit on the back of the head with a pancake. I whipped around to find my husband humming innocently, hands busy in the sink. This, of course, meant war. I picked that puppy up off the floor and hurtled it across the room at him. Back and forth it flew. He upped the ante the moment he grabbed whipped cream and smeared it in my hair.

It's always mid-way through these little rendezvous that I recall the fact that he always wins. *Always.* Not only is he bigger and stronger, but he's trained like a defensive tactics Jedi master. Pressure points, need I say more?

Memories of me flicking him with water years earlier flooded back to me. In response, he had pulled the spray hose from its place in the kitchen sink and hosed me in the face. I learned quickly that in playful combat, I was a defeat waiting to happen. But sneakiness...I could swing that.

So I snuck that chocolate pancake away and wrapped it in a pair of his clean underwear at the bottom of his drawer. A week later it showed up in my bedside table. Then back into his pile of shirts. Back and forth it went, for months. We didn't talk about it, it just quietly showed up in random spots throughout our room.

Funnily enough, this little chocolate pancake, while hard as a rock, never grew moldy. It simply snuck back and forth between his things and mine in our silent battle. A few weeks ago while purging our closet, I discovered it. It had fallen down the back of a pile of shirts, and so had removed itself from the game for several months. Straight back into his underwear drawer it went. Touché!

It is so true that the couple who pray together...and *play* together...stay together.

> "A cheerful heart is good medicine,
> but a crushed spirit dries up the bones"
>
> Proverbs 17:22

SAFE IN MY MOUTH

Something that has really helped protect the emotional intimacy of our marriage is what a friend once referred to as 'having their name be safe in our mouths'. While leading a small group many years ago, I had disclosed some personal information about another couple to her, not intending to spread gossip or speak ill of them, but simply to share a nugget of information *I* knew and *she* did not. I will never ever forget her response. *"You need to understand,"* she explained, *"that if you're willing to talk to me about them, that I'm left to assume you'll talk to them about me. And I need to know that my name is safe in your mouth."*

Her integrity and sensitivity totally transformed the way I viewed "innocent gossip" and set in motion a standard we hold fast to in our marriage. We will *never* gossip about each other to someone else, nor will we ever speak ill of each other in public.

My husband's name is safe in my mouth. And mine is safe in his. It's amazing the sense of safety and security this has reinforced between us, especially when going through times of tension and distance.

FEED YOUR SPIRIT

We have found along the way, as we've individually pursued a personal relationship with Jesus, and intentionally filled our tanks from the *true* source of satisfaction and meaning, that we're less apt to suck each other dry of the limited resources we have to give.

As a habitual multi-tasker, I maximize my time spent doing laundry by listening to podcasts (Kris Vallotton[2] and Steven Furtick[3] are my current favs). I listen to teaching series while on long road trips by myself, and intentionally carve out time to spend in one of the many excellent books available on personal development.

These little investments have proven to be incredibly beneficial, not just for my own personal growth and development, but also for what I bring into our marriage.

You've no doubt heard that it takes a village to raise a child. Well, we believe it takes a village to grow a healthy marriage. With that firm conviction propelling us, we've developed some incredibly close friendships with other couples with whom we now get to do life on a regular basis. We're part of a "tribe" of like-minded people, albeit wildly different, magnificently unique people, and I believe God intended life to be lived in this way.

We lead a small group that meets every other week, and on the off weeks, we take turns meeting as guys and girls. These weekly gatherings provide encouragement, accountability, wisdom, fellowship and fun. A sense of community we were created for, that our spouses alone cannot provide. Along with developing friendships in our local community and with other parents at our kids' school, we have discovered a mutual delight in pouring into the lives of those around us, and soaking in the beauty and diversity of those lives.

This is a glorious thing that, by default, fosters greater emotional intimacy in our own marriage.

TO THINE OWN SELF BE TRUE

It goes without saying that you cannot give away something you do not have. In the same way, we cannot truly love others, with all their faults and failures, until we've learned to love ourselves, with all of ours.

Find yourself, sweet friend. Who are you, really? What makes you tick? What fills your heart with passion and purpose? What is it you feel you could talk about forever?

What spiritual gifts, talents, and strengths do you have? How are you using them to fulfill your unique purpose in this world? You were knit together in your mother's womb for a divine purpose, and you're alive, today, for that reason. What is it, do you know?

Jon Acuff speaks to this in his book Quitter: *"More often than not, finding out what you love doing most is about recovering an old love or an inescapable truth that has been silenced for years, even decades...So instead of setting out to discover this thing you love doing, you've got to change your thinking and set out to recover it, maybe even rescue it."4*

Make it your mission to really get know who you are created to be and all you are uniquely crafted to accomplish, and then choose to love the *whole* package. Quirks, imperfections and all. When you do, you'll be able to express love to others from a healthier, more fully alive heart.

Do you realize that God uses even our failures and struggles for His glory? It's true. Our greatest mistakes are laced with opportunities for His goodness to shine through. I know. I'm the poster child for His ability to turn a mess into a message.

I don't want to spend my life being someone I'm not, nose to the ground, just trying to make it through. That is not the abundant life Jesus came to bring us.

When my heart is plump with wisely-sourced value, worth and purpose, not only is it contagious, but I free my hubby up to be who he's called to be in my life, and he in turn frees me. It also makes for great conversation starters when we have alone time together. We bounce ideas off each other, offer words of encouragement or wisdom, and fuel each other on in our great adventures.

When our eyes are fixed on Jesus and our arms linked with others, it's much harder to be robbed of our joy while traversing the obstacles and detours of life. We're focused and filled, rather than starved for affection and craving earthly fulfilment, which simply creates a vacuum of need and insecurity. And neither are endearing qualities in a spouse.

PLUG BACK IN

We cannot be selectively engaged in our marriages. We're either emotionally in, or we're out. We're also not responsible for the level of interaction our spouse provides. At the end of the day, we are responsible for our contribution alone.

When our life is all said and done, we get to choose what we're known for. I want to be recalled as a woman who loved her husband extravagantly. Not perfectly, but wildly. I want to leave a legacy of *love and grace*.

I don't want to get lazy in my relationship with my best friend. I want to be alive and fully-engaged in this adventure.

Carving out time to connect isn't easy, but without intentionally cultivating our emotional intimacy, our sexual intimacy will inevitably suffer.

Some may not understand the incredible burden I feel to be a sold-out, passionate wife who fiercely guards her husband's heart, and I think it's often due to the fact that submission flies in the face of this self-absorbed culture, and tends to be grossly misunderstood. But if pursuing something of worth that'll ripple into the lives of our children, and our children's children - even if misunderstood - earns me labels like "weak" or "old-fashioned," I'll own them.

I've had to ask myself whether I'm willing to look foolish in the eyes of this world, if it means having a marriage that honors the Father's heart? And I am.

I have lived this life long enough to know that I cannot try to please both man and God with my decisions, and really only One matters. We were created to live life for that audience of One.

Besides, as the saying goes, if we try to chase two rabbits, both will escape. So choose wisely in which direction to spend your energy.

We're the ones who eat the fruit of the choices we make, and when we get to enjoy the sweetness of the emotional intimacy we've worked hard to develop, it will prove to be well worth the effort.

While happiness is flimsy and circumstantial, creating a rich, wonder-filled life is possible in a Christ-centered marriage that chooses *joy in the everyday.*

REFLECTION & ACTION:

I've rounded up some questions for you and your hubby to tackle that will inspire conversation and cultivate emotional intimacy. Some of these questions are thought provoking and heart revealing, while others are simply light hearted and fun. They're broken into categories based on frequency; a few are worth asking on a weekly basis, while others are intended as more of an annual heart check-up.

WEEKLY:

- How have I communicated love and respect to you recently?
- How have I communicated a lack of love or respect to you recently?
- How can I pray for you, and help support you over the next week?
- Is there a Scripture or quote that you've read this week that especially stands out to you?
- Is there anything weighing on your heart that we need to discuss?
- If I could do one thing out of the ordinary that would really bless you this week, what would that be?
- What would make you feel sexually desired and appreciated this week?

MONTHLY:

- What would you really like for us to make time to do to-gether this month?
- How could I better meet your physical needs and de-sires?
- How could I better meet your emotional needs and de-sires?
- How can I help you be a better husband?
- How can I help you be a better father?
- Do you feel heard in our relationship?
- In what ways do we process frustration and disappoint-ment differently (inward/outward/internal/external), and how could we better communicate in this area by align-ing our styles?
- What gets your heart pumping and thrills you as you think about it?
- Where have you had a real victory this month? An area that your strengths have been evident?
- Where have you struggled this month? Is there an area that your weaknesses have been particularly evident?
- How do you feel our sex life is? What could make it bet-ter?

ANNUALLY:

- If money and time were not a factor, what would you do with your life?
- If you won the lottery, where would you go, and with whom?
- What is your favorite thing about yourself, personality wise?
- What is your favorite part of your body, and why?
- If there was one thing you could change about yourself, what would it be?
- What is your greatest fear?
- What is your biggest regret?

- What are your greatest strengths?
- What are some of your weaknesses?
- What is the most difficult loss you've ever suffered?
- How do you best receive my expression of love – through acts of service, quality time, gifts, words of affirmation, or through physical touch?
- What is a memory that you still have from childhood that stirs up heartache? Is there something about that memory that you feel you still need to process through or let go of?
- If there was one area of my personality or style of relating to you that – if I worked on it - would really bless you, what would it be?
- What do you find most attractive about me?
- Do you feel you have enough space to truly be you?
- What do I do that really irritates you?
- What spiritual gifts do you identify in me?
- How have you changed since we got married?
- In what area do you feel I've grown the most since we got married?
- What is one of your favorite memories of us?
- What is one thing you would like to accomplish, personally, over the next year?
- What is one thing you would like to see us accomplish, as a couple, this next year?
- Where do you see us in 5 years? 10 years? 20 years?
- What hobbies do you wish we could do together?

JUST FOR FUN:

- If there was a documentary filmed about your life, what would the title be, and what songs would you want included in the soundtrack?
- Have you ever laughed so hard that you peed a little in your pants?

- When you were younger, who was your biggest hero and why?
- Who is your greatest hero today?
- If you could have named yourself, what would you have chosen?
- If you won an all-inclusive vacation to anywhere in the world, where would you go?
- What is your earliest childhood memory?
- What are some of the things your parents taught you that you are thankful for today?
- What is something your parents said to you repeatedly, as a child, that you now find yourself saying to our kids?
- If you had the opportunity to establish one new law that everybody had to follow, what would it be?
- What did you want to be when you grew up?
- If you could start over, what would you want to do with your life?
- If you could share a meal with any Bible character, which one would it be?
- If you could have any super power, what would it be?
- If you could be alive during any period in history, when and where would you live?
- What is your all-time favorite book, and why?
- What is your all-time favorite movie, and why?
- Who is your favorite fictional character, and why?
- If you could eat only one food for the rest of your life, what would you choose?

"Do two walk together unless
they have agreed to do so?"

Amos 3:3

13

CHAPTER

SPIRIT MINGLER

We decided last summer to finally take on the task of tiling our kitchen floor. When we moved in over the summer of 2010, the kitchen boasted off-white linoleum with burgundy squares, soft pink counter-tops, a sexy rooster border, and burgundy walls - to complement the sponge-painted burgundy and pink living room it opened into. And I'm not talking "dusty rose," I'm talking the most offensive shade of "Pep-to-Bismol pink" you can imagine.

We painted the walls a fantastic shade of avocado green before we'd even closed on the house (which is another story for another day), and planned to install ceramic tile as soon as our bank account would allow it. Two years later, with the help of our tax return, it formally leapt onto our weekend to-do list.

The incredible men in our small group had offered to help install it, and seeing a couple of them actually knew what they were doing, we forged on with our plans. Everything was falling into place. With inexplicable delight, we headed to the store and picked out a beautiful 12 inch mottled gray-beige tile. Along with the impact it would have on the value of our home and the overall look of the kitchen, I remember walking out of the Menards, pushing a cart full of tile, cement board and grout, thinking..."*now I won't have to look at the smorgasbord of leftovers under the stools every time I don't feel like sweeping up after they eat.*"

I'm not kidding. I may love organizing, but I am one lazy housekeeper. I like to explain to people when they comment on how clean my house is, that there's a big difference between tidy, well organized and strategically laid-out...and *clean*. It's rarely the latter.

A year later and what's changed? Well, not much. There is still quite often a multi-course meal sampling on the floor beneath our counter stools...bran flakes, half-eaten noodles, sandwich crumbs, rogue peas...it's just that you can't see them unless you really look closely. They just sort of blend into the kaleidoscope of tile design. As a recovering perfectionist, I find this deeply satisfying. If I don't have to look at it, I'm happy. It's disgusting actually, if you think about it (which I try not to), but when it comes to sweeping up crumbs for the 37th time in one day...ignorance is indeed bliss.

New tile + same children with same barbarian eating habits = less noticeable overflow.

Hygienic? Not necessarily. Deceptive? I suppose. Convenient? You betcha.

Why am I boasting about my gorgeous tile while showcasing my appalling housekeeping habits? Because I think that when we build our marriages, and our families, on the right foundation - verses a convenient, artificial one - a lot of the junk that usually ruffles our feathers can be more easily overlooked. And let go of.

FOUNDATIONS

A grace-based approach to relationships covers a plethora of failure and shortcomings. And left-overs. Only, they're left-overs from past wounding, a chaotic season, and an uncertain future. Crumbs of an imperfect human existence in a broken world. The mess is a reality, but the way we look at it, and the way in which we deal with it, makes all the difference in a marriage.

Peter puts it this way in 1 Peter 4:8, *"above all, love each other deeply, because love covers a multitude of sins."*

We are multifaceted creatures, designed with a soul, spirit and body. As I mentioned at the beginning of the book, when one of those elements is hurting, the whole unit hurts. Sadly, because we're tangible human beings with a proclivity for tangible things, we tend to underestimate the power of the spiritual realm because it is rarely encountered with the naked eye. But when this world fades and our candy-wrapper bodies waste away, the treasures within - our spiritual beings - will remain. With this understanding, we're able to see that the spiritual realm is in fact more true and more real than the temporary physical realm.

What we build our marriages on *matters*. Foundations will make or break a structure. If we base our affection, commitment and loyalty solely on the chemistry we feel, then when our surging hormones transition after the first few years (or months), and our infatuation fades, our marriage will too.

When you strip away all the pomp and circumstance, if you have no Godly foundation, you're left with the daily grind. I don't know about you, but there is nothing appealing to me about simply running in the hamster wheel of suburbia. Rise, eat, work, be mom, be wife, eat, sleep, repeat.

I need something deeper. Something bigger than myself to reveal my mission, inspire my vision, fuel my passion, and woo me on to a greater purpose.

You were created for greatness. You have divine destiny wired into your being, and when you start to realize and develop your strengths and passions, and start discovering and unwrapping your unique contribution to this world, something incredible happens in the supernatural realm. Like we explored in the previous chapter, when you're living fully alive and wholeheartedly pursuing God's plan for your life, you impact the lives around you for *good*. It's right here that the world is transformed. One love-fueled interaction at a time.

Howard Thurman[1] speaks to this in his oft-quoted wisdom: *"Don't ask what the world needs. Ask what makes you come alive, and go and do it. Because what the world needs is people who have come alive."*

In fact, this is one of the things I find most attractive about my husband. It's when he's focused, missional-minded and gung-ho about something God has deposited in his heart. Watching him get excited about it, sharing his dreams and desires, he is never more alive than in these moments. And nothing is more sexy than a man who feels fully alive. As he talks about what he feels God is stirring in his spirit, his eyes literally light up.

His expectancy and hope is contagious, and this aligning of vision and Godly purpose cultivate a *spiritual* intimacy in our marriage.

Imagine how the world would be different if two people, pursuing wholeness and heaven-inspired purpose, tie the knot and go whole-hog after God's plan for them as a united, passionate force to be reckoned with.

Woah. The thought blows my mind! There is something so beautiful and inspiring and magnetic about people who have started to scratch the surface of destiny and who are beginning to understand why they were born for such a time as this.

PRESS IN

We love attending marriage conferences and series, and try to either attend or lead one each year. We also read a lot of books about marriage, although not always the same ones, and then we discuss what we're discovering and learning. I suppose we're killing two *literary* birds with one stone.

A really great way to develop your spiritual intimacy is to spend time reading the Bible together, or reading a couple's devotional. While we don't *consistently* do this, we have worked our way through a few of these, and our favorite one remains *Devotions for a Sacred Marriage* by Gary Thomas[2]. It's spiritually deeper than many we've read, is relevant and relatable, and always leaves us with something profound to chew on.

We have found that the sweetest seasons of our marriage have been ones that we've independently prioritized our relationship with the Lord, often motivating and challenging the other in the process, and as a result have grown closer to each other on the journey.

Picture a triangle standing on one of the sides as the base. God represents the apex of the triangle, and you and your spouse are at each of the lower angles. As you draw closer to God (up), spending time with Him and seeking His will for your life, you will - without even trying - draw closer to each other. By His brilliant design, that's just how it works.

The Bible explains it this way in Mathew 6:33 to *"seek first His kingdom and His righteousness, and all these things will be added unto you."*

Of course, praying together is one of the most significant moves you can make toward deeper spiritual intimacy, but boy is it easier to talk about than it is to actually flesh out. We used to think it was just us, but as we've mentored couples and talked with friends over the years, we've discovered there are actually very few couples who consistently, and easily, spend time in prayer together. But this is no reason to stop trying.

Taking a moment to quiet your hearts and talk with your Savior, together, is a precious thing. I wonder whether the difficulty involved in making this feel natural and become a consistent part of your day is indicative of how powerful and effective it is? Remember, the enemy attacks and disrupts what he's threatened by. So don't stop trying, even if it feels awkward. Just start small, and fumble your way through it together. God doesn't listen to our prayers with physical ears. He puts a stethoscope directly to our hearts, so even when the words don't emerge well assembled, he knows the cry of our heart.

I really believe praying *out loud* is more for *our* benefit than for some lofty spiritual purpose. Sometimes just hearing what's weighing on each other's hearts, in plain English - rather than scrambled brain chatter, allows us to better evaluate the problem and deal with the root issue, breathing life and encouragement into those deep places. It unites us for a common cause; locking shields and kicking the devil's butt.

One of the best ways to get comfortable with praying together is to pray as a family, with your little ones, before bed. Not only does it help you get comfortable with talking to God out loud, in an intentionally uncomplicated fashion, but it also models for your children the high value you place on prayer.

If you're feeling extra brave and *really* want prayer to rock your marriage, read on:

During the first marriage course we ever took, in our first year together, my hubby and I were told by the couple leading the group that there was something incredibly powerful about praying together before making love. They encouraged us to invite God into that time and in essence, dedicate our sexuality to him. At first we reeled a little, turning up our noses at the thought. "Gosh, how weird is that!"

But as we talked about it we realized that our response simply indicated a misunderstanding of God's heart on sex. We had, as I shared at the beginning of the book, failed to see the sacred link between sexual intimacy and its Creator. We had become so used to separating him from the act of sex that it seemed sacrilegious to intertwine the two. As if He'd blush being formally invited into the room, versus being there just because He always is.

As odd as it felt, they were right. Every single time we invited God into the midst of our intimacy and asked Him to bless it, there were fireworks. There was something mysterious and sweetly intoxicating about experiencing intimacy on such a heightened level of spiritual, emotional and physical sensitivity.

You may be thinking, "*Girl, you're crazy!*" but I dare you to try it. Double dog dare you.

Again, this is not something we do consistently, but there is really no good reason why we shouldn't. I think, much like praying together, it's easy to get into a routine, and breaking out of it - especially when it goes against the grain of your comfort level - tends to be avoided, even if unintentionally.

So let's commit to stepping out of our little boxes, shall we?

SOUL TIES

Great sex is about so much more than what lubrication you use, what position you assume, and how powerful your orgasm is. It's about the *intimacy*. Physical, emotional and spiritual intimacy. I believe that when we're sexually active with someone, even if only once, the effect of that union creates a powerful spiritual bond.

This is, I believe, a large part of why God instructs us to flee from sexual relationships outside of marriage. During a sexual experience, this powerful bond, or soul tie, is forged in the deepest parts of who we are and was actually designed to further cement your covenant. But when this bond is created outside of the safety of marriage it wreaks havoc, blazing a trail of shame and abandonment when the relationship comes to an end, because the tie that binds us to that person wasn't ever intended to be severed. There is no such thing as 'casual sex'. This bond is formed whether you want it or not. Fragments of our heart and soul cling to the heart and soul of the other person, and we are left feeling - accurately so - that pieces of us are missing.

Scripture explains the mystery of this soul bond like this, "*a man shall leave his father and his mother and shall cleave to his wife; and they shall be one flesh*"[3]. The Hebrew word translated as "cleave" is actually "to adhere"[4]. In essence, we create a "one flesh" union, literally one person glued to the other, that is designed to last a lifetime.

I remember my hubby and I intentionally praying together before we got married, breaking the power of those soul ties over our lives and asking God to fully restore us. It was so freeing, especially considering the incredible promiscuity of my past, and it enabled us to fully offer *all* of ourselves to each other, versus the left-over fragments of our souls.

"A person standing alone can be attacked and defeated, but two can stand back-to-back and conquer. Three are even better, for a triple-braided cord is not easily broken"

Ecclesiastes 4:12

WELCOME TO THE WAR

I believe that making love is one of the purest forms of worship and one of the most effective forms of spiritual warfare. A divinely inspired act of creativity, sex is far more powerful than we realize.

No wonder complacency, negativity and discontentment are foes we come face to face with regularly in the bedroom. If allowed, these subtle enemies will creep in and disable us at our very core, robbing us of our intimacy and connection, and eventually, our marriage.

We need to open our eyes and recognize this strategic plan that threatens to paralyze our purpose and suck the very life out of our marriages.

I'm sure you know already that you have an enemy. But did you realize, it's *not* actually your spouse?

It's an enemy whom Scripture paints in 1 Peter 5:8 as a lion on the prowl, *seeking* whom he can *devour.*

We're not talking "nibble" here, folks. *But devour.*

He hates love. For he is the very antithesis of love[5].

And you should know, he *hates* marriage. He is *intent* on distorting it, disenchanting it, *and ultimately, destroying* it.

Yours. And mine, to be exact.

Why? Because marriage is one of the most tangible expressions of God's extravagant love. I believe one of God's primary purposes for designing and introducing the concept of marriage to humanity was to paint for us a picture of His heart toward His people. Marriage is a theme we see woven throughout the Bible. Genesis opens with one in the story of Adam and Eve[6], and Revelation closes with one in the story of the Bridegroom (Jesus) and His bride (the church)[7].

It is a stunning picture that is constantly being smudged and distorted by the one who would rather we *not* comprehend this love. Marriage, as it was intended, illustrates the power of covenant and the beauty of selfless love and sacrifice.

John and Stasi Eldredge, in their book *Love & War*, explain how grasping this truth will help us understand why *"the fury of hell has been unleashed against [marriage]. God is telling a love story and the setting is war"*[8].

When trouble comes -- and it *will* come -- if we've built our marriage on the superficial pursuit of happiness, we're in trouble. We live in a world at war, not necessarily one fought with flesh and blood, but an epic battle in the spiritual realm.

It's easy to spot the warning signs of dysfunction in a marriage once they've manifested physically, but they almost always start at the spiritual level. When our spiritual intimacy is hampered -- or never developed -- our emotional intimacy will be limited, and our sexual intimacy will be crippled.

These layers of intimacy, while unique and powerful in their own right, are inseparable, and dysfunction in one of them will always result in a fractured connection in all.

We daily fight a battle that is waged against our marriages. Well...actually, we *can choose* to take a stand and fight, or we can continue on, *blindly*, getting whacked repeatedly in the back of the head with invisible ammunition.

Engage and fight *for* your marriage, or embrace apathy and fight *in* your marriage.

WHO ARE YOU AGREEING WITH?

A way we can actively fight for our spouse – rather than with them – is to ask God to put a guard on our minds and a filter on our mouths.

Choose to not make 'agreements' with the enemy of your soul regarding your spouse.

You know the ones...those little internal rants, most of them drenched in negativity, sarcasm and criticism...

"My husband is such a pig!"

"Why do I even try, he just wants one thing!"

"He doesn't appreciate anything I do for him"

"He's such a jerk...I should have known"

"I'll never open my heart to him again"

"He'll never change, this marriage is never going to work!"

It is imperative that we identify the origin and author of these thoughts, recognize the destructive plot going on behind the scenes, and refuse to allow them to take root in our hearts.

The Eldredges, in *Love & War*, go on to explain that when these little agreements linger, like *"tiny cracks in a structure,"* they have the potential to become something incredibly destructive. *"They might go away over time, but more often than not they become the beginnings of deeper fissures. Little cracks don't matter much in your sidewalk, but in other places they matter a great deal – like airplane wings, for instance, or the Hoover Dam. Places that will come under immense pressure. Like marriage"*[8].

We first learned about the concept of making agreements several years ago when we read Love & War and led the accompanying DVD series. Talk about an ah-ha! moment. With our eyes freshly aware of the negative chatter that plays constantly in our minds, we're able to more easily discern the author of those thoughts and nip the downward cycle in the bud. This has been huge for us.

It is not uncommon for one of us to approach the other after a time of disconnect and struggle, with a confession. *"Babe, I've been making some agreements about you, and our marriage, and I see now how this has brought further division. I've totally been believing lies and I'm so sorry. Please forgive me."* It's a hard act to pull off at first, and a humbling thing to admit, but it so quickly reestablishes connection and restores intimacy that it will quickly become your default resolution. The more we put on our big girl panties and do this, the easier it gets.

Humility and repentance are extraordinarily powerful.

Nothing sucks the air out of an argument like owning our role, extending a sincere apology, and requesting forgiveness.

I would encourage you, as you go through the day, to pay more attention to the chatter that plays in your head. So much of the poison that festers in our hearts and spews from our lips is a product of a simple 'seed' thought that's been planted. We agree with it, water it and nurture it, and then it grows out of control and explodes out of our mouths. Other times it simply causes us to withdraw completely, with our spouse left wondering what on earth has happened.

Nothing will squelch sexual intimacy like the weeds of bitterness and resentment.

Those little agreements are much like the door-to-door salesmen of old. When that doorbell rings, don't even open the door for them. If you let them over the threshold of your mind, they'll move right in, overhauling your whole house. Just say no, and replace that thought with a positive, life-giving one.

Remember that what you focus on *grows*. Guard your thoughts and be purposeful about turning even the slightest hint of a negative agreement into an opportunity for 'treasure hunting'. Intentionally focus on your husband's strengths and redeeming qualities, and you'll turn the tables on your enemy.

Now *that* is one satisfying maneuver.

LET HIM DO IT

One of the best things about building a spiritual foundation in your marriage, and diligently seeking out time, *individually and as a couple,* to grow and mature in your relationship with the Lord, is being able to watch God take care of things that are heavy on your heart, without having to whine or nag about it to your husband.

It's awfully tempting to want to usurp the Holy Spirit's role, praying out loud with great passion about our husband's character flaws, while preaching at them about areas of their life they need to work on, but "should"ing on them in the name of religious prowess will never accomplish anything good.

The problem is we misunderstand the Holy Spirit's purpose, and then do a pretty shoddy job of it to boot. He's patient and tender and firm and specific. He's called "the comforter" for a reason, and He approaches sin with a "here's the problem...and here's how we can fix it...let's go."

We, on the other hand, tend to attack our husbands with our interpretation of the problem, whine a whole lot, put the weight of our muddled emotions on them, and then practically beat them to death with a vague assessment of their character.

Not very effective in wooing a heart change, is it?

When we offer up whispers of prayer and petition to God instead of hurtling accusation and criticism toward our husbands, a desire for growth has room to sprout in them, and in us.

Love compels us, it empowers change and motivates reconciliation, while fear and accusation simply create distance and foster resentment. And sadly, love doesn't tend to be our word-vehicle of choice.

While we do, as wives, get to play an instrumental role in our husband's lives when it comes to accountability and intercession, conviction and correction are not our responsibility.

When we let the Holy Spirit do his thing, it's powerful and effective!

There have been many times an issue has weighed on my heart and I've had to choose whether to take matters into my own hands, or whether to patiently talk to God about it, asking Him to correct my hubby's heart and then leave it at His feet. Don't confuse this process with my original method of stuffing frustration and passive-aggressively stewing.

Because of my constant self-talk, I can easily get all worked up about something that really isn't a big deal, and then when the opportunity arises to talk to my husband about it, I explode, spitting accusations, and promptly fall apart.

But when I love him through the tough stuff, hard as it may be, choosing rather to take my concerns to his Creator, my hubby will often seek me out to initiate reconciliation with a tender heart because *God* stirred something in him and he knew it needed to be corrected.

Sure, this isn't always the way "intense fellowship" is handled in our home, nor does this unique 'Holy Spirit download approach to conflict' always resolve in the time frame that I wish it would, but with a little self-discipline and patience, a messy blow-up is averted, and our spiritual intimacy is enhanced.

Don't be discouraged if this feels far from possible in your marriage. While I believe this response *does* depend greatly on the spiritual maturity and sensitivity of our men, it is *always* beneficial to go to God *first*. I have learned that *timing* and *tone* play a tremendous role in getting a problem hashed out and solved amicably, and God handles my raw emotion far better than my husband does. Getting 'prayed up' on *my* end always helps to diffuse a potentially explosive conversation by equipping me with the grace and wisdom I desperately lack at times, while allowing God to give me His perspective and His heart for my husband.

DIVINE DISAPPOINTMENT

My four year old son has his heart set on marrying Elsa. Yes, that would be the Disney queen of Arendelle from the movie Frozen. Every time he sees her picture or hears "Let It Go", he begs me, *"Please mom...I just want to marry Elsa!"* Despite my best efforts to dissuade him, or to enlighten him to the unlikelihood of this matrimonial possibility, he won't budge. While we may not be this naive in our understanding of marriage, and may have a better handle on reality, I think we can set ourselves up for disappointment in much the same way.

We have great expectations coming into marriage and seem surprised when we find ourselves feeling disappointed and alone, eating a pint of Ben & Jerry's and watching *27 Dresses* for the umpteenth time.

Disappointment shows up in that space between what we expected marriage to look and feel like, and what we're experiencing.

This may come as a surprise to you, but every single human relationship was designed by God to leave us wanting. Yes, even our marriages. No matter how healthy and vibrant our connection, there will always be a hunger and thirst for something more that our husband will remain incapable of satisfying.

Our spouse was never designed to complete us. Complement us, yes, but fully complete us? No.

I realize that if you're a hardcore Jerry Maguire fan you may be tempted to throw this book across the room while muttering, *"But he had me at hello"* under your breath, but hear me out for a minute.

When we were created, we were designed with a 'God-shaped' hole. Try as we might to fill that void with status, sex, money, drugs, and materials things, nothing will ever satisfy that vacuum in our souls like the One who was designed to fill it.

> *"It is a foolish woman who expects her husband to be to her that which only Jesus Christ Himself can be: always ready to forgive, totally understanding, unendingly patient, invariably tender and loving, unfailing in every area, anticipating every need, and making more than adequate provision"*[9]

> *Ruth Graham Bell*

Expectations can be an incredibly destructive force when placed on a relationship. You may be relieved to find out that we're not actually called to live with lofty *expectations*, but are simply invited to live with a sweet *expectancy* of God's goodness fleshed out through his beautiful, though broken, creation. There's a big difference, and embracing this lifestyle will make all the difference in your marriage.

Even within marriage, we can shift from looking to our husbands to *reaffirm* our value, worth and beauty in a healthy way - to expecting them to *define us*. We all ache to belong, to be loved and to be fully known, but as long as we place that burden on our husbands to bear, rather than on our God, those deep places will remain unsatisfied and will drive us to search for significance elsewhere.

Our sexual connection can become strained because we feel deeply disappointed and hurt by our husbands' inability to meet those needs.

While we may top each other's 'love tank' up, acting more as a supplement than a main course, we are broken vessels incapable of completely filling each other up. After all, *we cannot give what we do not have.*

You cannot fill your husband's cup, and he cannot fill yours, but we can, together, go to the *source.*

THE SCULPTOR

One of the most divine purposes of marriage is not to define us, but to *refine* us. To transform us more and more into the likeness of Christ.

I heard a story of a famous sculptor who was asked by someone who'd stopped to admire his work, how it was that he was able to so beautifully extract a statue of a horse from a block of marble. The sculptor smiled and responded, *"Why, it's easy! I simply look at it from this angle, and from that angle...and then again from this angle, and finally I just chip away everything that's not horse."*

Sounds simple enough, doesn't it? To someone who knows what he's doing!

And this is what God is in the process of doing in us. He's chipping away everything that's not Jesus in us. And it just so happens that one of the sharpest, pointiest tools in His hand bears a striking resemblance to our husband.

Fancy that.

Remember, God is more concerned with our *character* than our *comfort*[10]. And while marriage is glorious, it can also be mighty uncomfortable at times. Which makes it the perfect incubator for character development.

When I allow the Lord to fill me and establish my identity, letting Him take my insufficiency and inadequacy, and in exchange giving me His sufficiency, and taking my lack of confidence and in its place depositing a supernatural God confidence, I position myself in the perfect place to *receive* and *give* love. Not in spite of my brokenness, but because of it. When we take our cracked pots to the only One who's fully capable of knowing and loving and filling us completely, we overflow that peace and joy onto those around us. His love leaks out of the cracks and crevices and nourishes those other leaky vessels in our lives.

When we realize that our spouse wasn't intended to complete us, we take those core needs to the only One who can satisfy them, and free our marriage to be what it was intended to be.

One of my favorite Scripture verses is Isaiah 43. In verse 2 it says, "*When you pass through the waters, I will be with you; and when you pass through the rivers, they will not sweep over you. When you walk through the fire, you will not be burned; the flames will not set you ablaze.*"

The Bible doesn't mince words about tough times. They *will* come. But we are also guaranteed that when they do come, we will not be alone. When it feels like your world is falling apart, cling to the unshakable One. When you start smelling smoke and find your marriage in the fire, press in to each other, and press in to God. Refuse to allow crisis to tear you apart, but allow God to use the heat to refine you and mold you more into His likeness.

At the end of the day, your spiritual intimacy will hold you together, and if you're willing to step out and trust Him with your everything, you'll come out on the other side with your hearts knit more closely together and your faith stronger than ever.

REFLECTION & ACTION:

- What might be hampering your spiritual intimacy with your spouse? Is God stirring anything in your spirit that may need to be dealt with?

- Pray and ask God to reveal any lingering soul ties from your past, ask Him to break their power over your life and to restore your wholeness so you can fully offer yourself to your spouse.

- Is there someone or something that you and your husband could commit to pray for -- sometimes having a prayer focus, a person or organization to prayerfully support, makes it less awkward to explore the practice of praying together.

- As there tends to be a theme, or pattern, to the agreements we make in our minds, what agreements do you find yourself making regularly about your husband? Commit to start agreeing with what God says about your man, rather than what your mutual enemy has to say.

- Next time you feel your hackles rising up and are tempted to jump down your husband's throat because of a trend you're seeing in his behavior, try taking it to the Lord in prayer and asking Him to deal with your heart first (sometimes the way we react to something is because there's something deeper going on that we need to process through and uproot), and then deal with your husband's heart.

- Where have you placed expectations on your husband, to meet core needs in your life, that only God can meet? How might your relationship change if you let your husband off the hook, and freed him to be who he was created to be? How might your life change if you in turn pursued the only One who could deeply satisfy those unmet needs?

- What small steps can you take this week to cultivate a deeper sense of spiritual oneness in your marriage?

7 DISCUSSION STARTERS
to help cultivate spiritual intimacy in your marriage:

1. When I thank God for you, the characteristics or qualities I focus on are...

2. What 3 Christ-like qualities do you see in me?

3. How has tapping into God's power broken strongholds in our marriage?

4. What recent hardship we've experienced have you been able to see God's fingerprints in?

5. Do we allow God to use our strengths, and our weaknesses, as a couple to bless and encourage others? How could we do this better?

6. How can we help each other become more authentic in our relationship with Jesus and our expression of that faith?

7. Where might God be asking us to step out and take a risk together?

"Rejoice always, pray continually,
give thanks in all circumstances;
for this is God's will for you in Christ Jesus."

1 Thessalonians 5:16-18

14

CHAPTER

FIFTY SHADES OF COUNTERFEIT

When I was eighteen, I got a job at an upscale, privately owned restaurant just off the highway in Okemos. Think pretty mauve napkins folded into fanciful shapes, polished silverware, live piano music and $200 tips from pharmaceutical reps. It was surprisingly hard work that paid extremely well; which was convenient seeing I had to buy the most expensive shoes I've ever purchased in my entire life simply to keep my tarsals from spontaneously combusting mid-shift.

One night, while closing after a double shift, a middle-aged couple slipped in for dinner at the very last minute. After getting an okay from the chef, I seated and served them. By this point in the night, most of the kitchen staff and servers had gone home. I was the official host, server, bartender, busboy and bottle washer, and had been working since 10 that morning. My feet and back were killing me and it was taking every ounce of grace I could muster to not chew their cha-teaubriand for them and shove it down their throats with the back of a fork.

Needless to say, their request for dessert and coffee almost sent me into cardiac arrest. Could they possibly drag this night out any longer?

Grabbing the dessert tray from the giant kitchen cooler, I showcased our sweet treats for the night; caramel crème brulee, tiramisu, vanilla bean ice-cream with a chocolate ganache, and a triple berry mousse with custom-piped chocolate fleur-de-lis. All whipped up daily by our very own pastry chef and all probably more fantastically named than I recall.

He went with coffee, while she opted for the vanilla bean ice-cream. Thankful to have the end in sight, I grabbed a cup of freshly brewed coffee, snagged her beautifully smothered dessert from the tray, and headed out for my final run.

In hindsight, I am somewhat horrified to admit that I did this. Partly because it's sloppy service to not use fresh ingredients when assembling a dessert at such a classy restaurant, but mostly because any semi-smart human being would have known that ice-cream would in fact no longer be ice-cream if stored in a cooler. I'll blame it on the 12 hour shift. Or may-be it was the constant food fog that accompanied such a long day, what with our proximity to freshly baked bread and gorgonzola crumbles.

When the lady waved me down, I assumed it was to request the check so they could finally go away. But no. Apparently she wanted to inform me that I had tried to feed her a ginor-mous ball of butter, sprinkled with cinnamon, and drowned in chocolate syrup. And she wasn't very impressed.

Darn it.

Not my finest moment as far as restaurant memories go, registering second only to the night I set my hand on fire making cherries jubilee under a ceiling fan.

Sexual counterfeits are much like that beastly scoop of buttery badness; they may appear to satisfy, and are certainly quick and easy alternatives to the real thing, but they always leave us wanting; pathways clogged, hearts feeling greasy.

When we base our decisions solely on how things *look* or *feel*, or seek out convenience and comfort over quality and service, everyone comes up short.

Instant gratification will get us every time; we forfeit what we want *most*...for what we want *now*. Especially when it comes to sexually charged encounters. It's hard to swim upstream in a society that sings, *"if it feels good, sounds fun, and appears to be relatively harmless right up front, why not give it a whirl?"* If 'celebrity' doctors claim something is normal, healthy even, why deny ourselves? After all, wouldn't God want us to be happy and satisfied?

But herein, sweet sister, lies the problem: if we don't dig deeply enough into what it is we're dipping into *before* sinking our teeth into it, or carefully weigh the consequences of the choice we're about to make *before* clicking 'enter', we dabble in things that swallow us whole before we even realize what has hit us.

We may intend to try just a morsel, but arousal is a mysterious thing, and it leaves us undone. It's a powerful, intoxicating, God-created experience, yes, but an awfully reckless tour guide. It will devour you from the inside out if allowed to run rampant or unchecked.

Not wielded wisely or God-yielded consistently, it forms habits, and habits give way to addiction. And you see, addiction is a stealthy dictator. Subtle at first, greedy and merciless in the end. We seldom realize we're addicted to something until it's too late.

It may look glamorous and fun on its way into the room, and that temporary rush of adrenaline it provides is thrilling...but it leaves us feeling exhausted, exposed and vulnerable on its way out.

Only, it doesn't actually leave. It just sucks us dry and spits us back out, over and over again. And when no one else talks about the danger and devastation and depravity of the pit we feel stuck in, we suffer in silence. Feeling very much alone.

We were not designed to be ruled and guided by an endless search for pleasure. Satisfaction wasn't ever intended to be our chief motivator.

What was created to be a beautiful by-product of a healthy, unselfish relationship, has become a core objective in relationships. *Meet my needs, or I'll find someone, or something, else that can.*

We've watched several marriages around us crash and burn because one, or both, decided to take their search for sexual satisfaction out of the safety of their marriage covenant.

Please know that while I don't want this chapter to come across as accusatory or judgmental in any way, I do feel an incredible burden to candidly and honestly peel back the veil on pornography, masturbation and erotic fiction. While these may be controversial topics, even within the four walls of the church, I trust you'll hear my heart, and take a peek at the info below before you mentally check out. And then, we can simply agree to disagree if you're not buying it. But I urge you to not allow your hackles to rise and to throw the baby out with the proverbial bathwater before reading what I have to say.

While affairs may seem like the most obvious issue to tackle in this section -- and they most certainly are a blatant counterfeit to marital intimacy -- they don't tend to be the initial step in the wrong direction. I don't have any facts or statistics to back me up here, but I would wager that a more subtle counterfeit which no longer provides the necessary level of satisfaction, acts as the gateway to such an encounter.

PORNOGRAPHY

You see, pornography is an insidious cancer that is growing rampantly in the soul of our society. It may appear harmless, but it's the furthest thing from it.

The *problem* with porn and masturbation is actually part of their appeal; *they're a quick fix*. With the relational dimension completely removed, intimacy is whittled down to nothing more than a self-serving sex act. Sure, it's quicker and less complicated -- which, in this microwave age, is how we like to roll -- but this convenience comes at a tremendous cost. Because it's completely devoid of any emotional connection or investment, it's the equivalent of living off sexual McDonald's, when fine dining is just around the corner. Sure, it may require more of an investment if you decide to go the sophisticated route, but there is just no substitute for the nourishment and connectedness that is cultivated in that time spent together, naked and vulnerable.

In bed, not at a restaurant, just in case that needed clarifying.

When we engage in sexual activity, a flood of chemicals surge through our bodies. Dopamine, norepinephrine, testosterone, oxytocin and serotonin[1] all play a part in the stunning crescendo of an orgasm and, when experienced within the intimacy of marriage, they aid in further bonding a couple; body, mind and spirit. If sex was designed to be a wildly intimate connection between a husband and wife, once the emotional connection is removed, you're left with empty flesh.

Eventually that flesh becomes an insatiable beast that will literally destroy itself to reach the next level of satisfaction.

When we indulge in pornography -- be it movies, magazines or novels -- we set off a neurochemical firestorm in our brain. These chemicals then carve out pathways that, over time, need more frequency and more stimulation to achieve the same response. We are, by design, creatures of habit, and the patterns we establish (sexually) influence and ultimately dictate our behavior.

Remember the days when guys had to trek down to those seedy joints in the shady parts of town to snag a magazine or a VHS if they wanted a fix? Now it comes looking for them on every mobile device. They used to be able to avoid getting into trouble by simply choosing to not search for x-rated sites. Today, our poor husbands get inundated by the adult entertainment industry on a daily basis. And our sons have 4th grade buddies with smart phones. And those buddies have older brothers with porn under their beds.

Our men can no longer stay 'pure' by default. It takes incredible commitment, determination, self-control and accountability. Day in, and day out.

The heart-breaking fact is, most every male either has been exposed to porn, or already has a problem with it. And by 'problem', I mean addiction.

According to a study done by Covenant Eyes in early 2014, 68% of young men and 18% of women use porn at least once every week[2].

Here are some other startling statistics from that report:

- The porn industry generates $13 billion each year in the U.S.
- Internet porn alone is a $3 billion per year business.
- 67% of young men and 49% of young women say viewing porn is an acceptable way to express one's sexuality.
- According to an analysis of more than one million hits to Google's mobile search sites, more than 1 in 5 searches are for pornography on mobile devices.
- 50% of all Christian men and 20% of all Christian women say they are addicted to pornography.
- 51% of pastors say Internet pornography is a possible temptation.
- 9 out of 10 boys were exposed to pornography before the age of 18.
- 35% of boys say they have viewed pornographic videos "too many times to count."
- The American Academy of Matrimonial Lawyers reports that 56% of divorce cases involve one party having "an obsessive interest in pornographic websites."
- 88% of scenes in porn films contain acts of physical aggression, and 49% of scenes contain verbal aggression.

It is no longer a debate. It's a simple truth: pornography is a destructive, mind-altering, body-objectifying drug, and it's spreading like wild fire.

I remember several years ago having a heart-naked conversation with a friend who had, in so many words, divulged her husband's porn habits. She tried, at first, to make it sound as though it didn't matter to her, and that he was "*just being a guy,*" after all...it "*took some of the pressure off*" her, but I could tell simply by looking at her face, and the way her frame sank, that it crushed her. When it came up again in conversation, a few weeks later, she broke. Weeping, she asked, *"Am I not enough for him, Joy?"*

It's the burning question on the heart of every woman whose husband struggles with porn. *Is who I am, and what I have to offer you, not enough?*

While you may be thinking, *"Okay, why are you telling me all this...I already know how devastating and destructive porn addiction is, thanks to my husband's battle,"* I believe it's possible to become numb to the heart-ache and reluctantly embrace the problem as "normal." But don't give up. And please, don't give *in*.

It's easy to write pornography off as a "man's problem," and statistically speaking, men *are* more drawn to graphic, image-driven porn, but women are by no means immune. I know this from personal experience, and it's not an easy habit to break, nor is it a comfortable confession to make.

While we may not be lured in by the same bait, the arousal it elicits deep within us keeps us coming back.

I distinctly remember watching porn for the first time when I was 13. While my parents house-sat for another family, I sifted through their videos in the basement. I'll never forget being caught off guard by the way my little body responded to it. And then again, in the darkest seasons of my struggle with promiscuity (between the age of 15 and 18), I was exposed to porn repeatedly.

While I hadn't sought it out initially, my heart and body had become so numb to the act of sex, that the arousal porn and masturbation elicited in me made me feel a little more human. And a little less dead inside. As is the nature of the beast, this set in motion a hunger for more, and by the time I was 17, I was hooked.

Along with the habitual trap of pornography, comes the struggle to then reengage intimately with a loved one[3].

If trust hasn't been completely severed, and space is still being created for intimacy in the marriage, the battle to maintain sexual performance begins.

Once our bodies become conditioned to respond a certain way (remember those chemicals that fire when watching porn?), reaching orgasm during a healthy sexual encounter becomes considerably harder[4]. In addition to battling premature ejaculation and other possible erectile dysfunction[5], men tend to develop unrealistic expectations of their wife's body and performance, and a narcissistic, self-centered approach to sex is established[6].

After inundating the pleasure centers in the brain and indulging in instant gratification for so long, they actually damage their ability to engage and perform intimately with a *real* human being. The likelihood of being able to emotionally remain present and engaged, rather than flipping through the myriad of mental images seared into their minds, becomes virtually impossible.

They've outsourced their pleasure centers only to discover they now require those novelties for arousal. As a result, the joy of connection is diminished and true intimacy is destroyed by the counterfeit.

Marital intimacy, and all the glory it carries, was designed to require the laying aside of self, and the giving of ourselves to the other. With reckless abandon. But you see...we're not two dimensional centerfolds. We're complex, and mysterious, and oh, so wildly different from each other (refer to chapter 8). We require wooing, and priming, emotional connection, time, and trust, and THEN we come alive. It is not for the faint of heart. Or the lazy.

A few years ago, a precious friend shared with me that her husband appeared to no longer be interested in sex. While this situation is the extreme end of the spectrum, she -- along with a handful of other women in my life -- is a rare find; they actually have *higher* sex drives than their husbands. I keep hoping they can lay hands on me and impart some of their magical libido into my veins, but it has yet to happen.

As my friend and I sat, teary eyed, sipping our coffee, she seemed convinced that a midlife crisis was to blame for his lack of interest. I, however, was not. She went on to explain what had happened the night before. After putting their little one down to sleep, she had dressed up in a sexy little number, and slipped downstairs to woo him from his perch in front of the TV. He looked at her, rolled his eyes, and sighed. She ended up back upstairs, alone, and crying herself to sleep. His blatant rejection of her was becoming a trend and was chipping away at her confidence and self-esteem. I knew pornography and masturbation were at the root of his detachment when she mentioned his response to her seduction attempt the night before. *"Why spend thirty minutes trying to have an orgasm with you when I can take care of it in 5 minutes by myself?"* Oh, how my heart broke at the sight of this beautiful woman utterly *undone* by her husband's callous response.

This is the true face of sexual perversion. Not the pretty one we see on the call card, but the shattered countenance of the one left behind.

It astounds me how the group of men who *appear* to no longer be interested in sex, is growing. Not because they're genuinely *not* interested in sex, but because porn addiction -- either past or present -- has ruined their appetite for the real thing.

Great sex *demands* that we become a student of each other, that we create space for honest communication, and allow time to play.

Let me just say, to those just starting out on the marriage journey, that when you put the effort in...it just. gets. better. I remember asking my mom, who had been married to my dad for 30 years when we tied the knot, how they kept the spark alive. How had it not become boring? Her response was simple and surprising. *"Oh love...it just gets better with time."* I thought she was delusional. But 10 years into this gig, I echo her response. It just gets better.

We've spent the last 10 years learning what makes the other one tick. What we like, and what we don't. What makes us feel loved and treasured, and what deflates our spirits. We've seen the value of speaking each other's love languages, even when they're not our own. We've created a safe place to share where we're struggling, where vulnerability and transparency come naturally. We've discovered what turns the other one on, and what positions work like a charm. We've also figured out short-cuts for when creativity is necessary. We've grown so much over the past decade, but we've grown *together*, and that has made all the difference between the sheets.

There's no 30 day plan or quick-fix substitute for good old fashioned time spent investing in each other.

But throw in the busyness that has become our new norm, the many hats we wear and plates we spin, the chaos of family life, and the way in which society sees monogamy as restricting, and it's no wonder porn and masturbation have become so widely accepted and celebrated. It's become all about *me* and *my* satisfaction.

You may be wondering about watching porn together as a form of foreplay. Isn't it fine if it's not done in secret? Sure, it'll temporarily boost your libido and heat your sheets for a few nights, but at what cost? Study after study reveals that, along with the effects I mentioned above (which hold true whether you watch by yourself or as a couple), pornography chips away at the foundation of a marriage, decreases sexual satisfaction, fuels distrust and insecurity, and actually increases the likelihood of divorce[6].

Prolactin is one of those feel-good chemicals that, along with oxytocin, course through your system after making love and it leaves us feeling more content and attached to our spouse. In a study done at the University of Paisley in Scotland, some subjects had sex with their partner, while others masturbated to porn. Afterward, there was 400% more prolactin in the bloodstream of the subjects who had made love.[7]

So, why settle for a destructive counterfeit when the real thing is so much better?

MASTURBATION

So, what's the big deal with masturbation and why did I lump it into this category? Well, because they tend to go hand-in-hand, and because I truly believe it's a counterfeit. It, too, masquerades as a harmless exploration of self, but ends up in the same self-obsessed cesspool as porn.

It's a slippery slope, this little habit, and is usually indicative of a deeper heart issue. While there are people I respect within the Christian community who have differing opinions to me on this subject, here's my take on it:

While Scripture doesn't specifically spell out masturbation as a sin, it does make a few things pretty clear.

1 Corinthians 6:13 and 1 Thessalonians 4:3-5 express the importance of us abstaining from sexual immorality and practicing self-control, and Matthew 5:28 talks plainly about God's stance on lust. I don't know about you, but it's pretty hard to masturbate with a pure mind. Masturbation may not be listed as its own category of sin, but lust sure is, and it's rather impos-

sible to pull one off without the other.

If we're told our bodies are not our own[8], and that sexuality is not about self[9] ...try as we might, how *do* we justify it?

I really do believe our relationship with God isn't about rules and religion, but about freedom and relationship. But with that being said, it's up to us to manage our freedom. As Paul so aptly says in 1 Corinthians 6:12, *all things are permissible, but not everything is beneficial.*

So in regards to masturbation, I think it's wise to ask ourselves a few questions:

- How does it *truly* benefit us? Yes, self-discovery and exploration are important parts of learning what makes you purr, but that is something your husband should be a part of.
- How does it glorify God? We are, after all, called to glorify Him in everything we do. And a vibrant, well-prioritized sex life does just that.

- How does it enrich your marriage? Masturbation is a poor substitute for the real thing, and simply feeds the self-gratifying mindset we're trying to kill.

It's interesting just how quickly masturbation rewires your brain and body to respond to a particular thought, sight or touch. Once your body becomes accustomed to arousal and orgasm through that particular method -- typically devoid of any emotional connection -- it becomes harder to respond sexually to anything outside of that[10].

Much like the effects of porn on marriage, what appears to be a convenient, risk-free 'practice', only complicates an already complex exchange.

As a side note, because I know there are times that life gets busy and we struggle to connect...if it's been a while since we've made love and my hubby is struggling, he has committed to let me know. We then make a point of connecting sexually as soon as humanly possible. By handling it this way, I know I'm doing my part to guard his heart from temptation, he's honoring me by being honest and vulnerable about where he's at, and it buys us a little more time to carve out a date for some *real* fireworks.

We feel pretty strongly about full disclosure and transparency. To us, it's a matter of integrity, and it has the potential to protect, or without it, to destroy, our marriage. When we had been married for just a few months, I vividly recall my hubby sharing with me one day that he had been wrestling with sexual thoughts and feelings for one of my closest friends. It absolutely *wrecked* me. I immediately wanted to push that friend out of my life, and was so hurt by my hubby's confession that I shut down to him sexually.

I then did the smartest thing I could have done. I went to my mom and poured out my heart and I'll never forget her words of wisdom. She urged me to be extra careful in my response to my hubby when he's baring his heart and sharing his struggles. I had communicated -- in that angry visceral response -- that it was *not* safe for him to bare his soul to his best friend. He had approached me reluctantly, hoping I would lift him up in prayer and hold him accountable, and I'd shamed him. I realized, after that tearful conversation with my mom, that if I could respond to conversations like this with grace and understanding, I would nurture the safety of our relationship and he would continue being open and transparent with me.

I could choose to be shocked and hurt and angry, or I could choose -- tough as it may be in the moment -- to be compassionate, understanding and honored by his integrity and passion for purity. I've chosen the latter. And ever since that realization, 9 years ago, my hubby *knows* he can come to me when he's struggling. If life has been busy and we haven't carved out time for intimacy, he will be particularly vulnerable to the temptation that is out there. And boy, is it out there when you're a smokin' hot baldy in uniform. So in knowing the condition of his heart (and hormones), I can do *my* part to protect him and guard his mind against temptation. Bam! Smart cookie, that mother of mine.

Believe it or not, sexual intimacy within marriage is not only a form of spiritual warfare, but is a powerful act of worship that glorifies the author of this gift.

I really believe one of the greatest dangers of experimenting in the gray area of masturbation is the focal shift that inevitably occurs. As we get sucked further into the desire-gratify-crave cycle, we move from pursuing intimacy with our spouse to elevating the gift of sexuality to a point that it now overshadows the *mutual* participation and enjoyment of sex. We shift from worshipping the Giver by celebrating His gift, to worshipping the gift.

Humans are hardwired for worship, and if we're not careful, we easily transition into worshiping the *created*, rather than the *Creator*.

So in short, it's not about rules and laws. It's about wisdom and stewardship. Sure masturbation provides a euphoric experience, but so does cocaine. I rest my case.

> *"True happiness... is not attained through self-gratification, but through fidelity to a worthy purpose"*[11] Helen Keller

ROMANCE NOVELS

So, what about erotica? Smutty romance novels are, by and large, a women's sexual drug of choice. Referred to as "mommy porn," they fly off the shelves and quietly slip into the Kindle cart because we just can't seem to get enough.

Just look at the way Fifty Shades of Grey glorified the world of BDSM[12] by turning a manipulative, controlling sex addict into a romantic hero.

I'm really *not* trying to come off as a prude here. I get the draw of this stuff, I really do. The first time I stumbled upon erotic fiction, I was 10 years old and had snuck off with a book my older sister had taken out of the library. I sat quietly in the bathroom reading...shocked, door locked, heart racing, legs squeezed awkwardly together. I had no idea what I was experiencing, but that physical response awakened something in me that craved more. While I didn't get lured into romantic novels the way I did into porn (quite possibly because I hated reading, until I discovered Mary Higgins Clark at the age of 16), I flirted with the possibility after I got married, during seasons of particularly low sex drive.

It seems logical enough. With sexperts raving about the benefits of Hilary Home-maker indulging in erotica, and all the raving testimonies of middle-aged women jump-starting their libidos by simply reading a naughty book, it's tempting to give it a whirl.

"If it arouses me, which -- Lord knows is a miracle these days -- and increases my desire for sex, my husband will be thrilled ...so it must be beneficial to my marriage," we reason.

But we're setting ourselves up for failure in much the same way graphic porn sets our husbands up. Once those words have formed images and cemented themselves into your memory, it's incredibly hard to get them out. And then in a moment of intimacy, in the same way visual porn takes your husband's mind away from *you*, erotica draws your mind away from your husband.

You end up discovering that your husband -- alone -- no longer does it for you, which fuels your need for more romance novels. And the cycle begins.

In much the same way those artificial, air-brushed babes reprogram our hubby's expectations of us, and our bodies, romance novels rewrite our hopes and expectations of our husbands -- and their bodies. Or should I say, their knowledge of *our* bodies.

May I just say, romantic movies drive me nuts for the same reason. The sex scenes are so incredibly unrealistic and, just like everything we've explored here, they create unrealistic expectations for the viewer. Since when does the average woman groan that much during sex, climax that quickly, and not have to reach for a wad of Kleenex to clean-up afterwards? Real sex is messy and complicated, and yes, occasionally awkward and disappointing. But considering no one would actually pay to watch that scene, Hollywood pumps up the experience, packages it neatly, and leaves us feeling unsexy, squishy and boring.

As long as our minds are off reenacting scenes we've read or watched, in a hopes to engage more passionately, we'll check out of the moment with *our* men, and step into someone else's fictional encounter. As we've discovered earlier in this book, great sex is about so much more than a physical exchange. When we're not able to be emotionally and mentally present with our husbands during intimacy, we've forfeited a tremendous amount of the purpose and power of sex.

Besides, real men don't need ropes and chains to make their women feel undone and conquered in the best of ways.

ADDICTION

"A new study has revealed that YOU are the reason you can't lose weight." I literally laughed out loud when I heard this on the radio a few days ago. Yup, I sure am. As much as we'd all like to blame McDonalds for making us fat, it's often a blatant lack of self-control that has got us into the predicaments we find ourselves in today.

We tend to think of an addict as someone who's strung out on heroin or fiercely attached to their daily six-pack of Budweiser with a whiskey chaser. But addiction is far more clandestine than that.

Merriam-Webster defines addiction as "the state of being enslaved to a habit or practice or to something that is psychologically or physically habit forming." It's pretty clear-cut, isn't it?

So while you won't get the shakes if you go without porn for 2 weeks, nor -- as Mark Gungor candidly puts it -- will any headstone ever read, "*Failure to Ejaculate*" as a means of death[13], it's important to realize that the pleasure cycles set in motion by these habits can be as hard to break as a full-blown drug addiction. As someone who has personally wrestled with more covert 'addictions' in my teenage years, hear my heart when I say, "*Be careful what you invite into your hidden life.*" Your battle may be fought behind closed doors, where labels like 'crackhead' and 'alcoholic' aren't tossed around...but the fight is as brutal. And just as destructive to your marriage.

It's a high cost war, beloved, and not one worth fighting. The battle wounds remain tender, and the roots that burned images into your heart run deep and wild. Even if the struggle occurred years ago, sexual secrets have a way of holding you hostage. When kept in the dark, they have power over you. When brought into the light, you gain power over them.

Awakening it and getting acquainted with our sexuality is a beautiful thing, don't get me wrong. God created us as sexual beings, and desires that we experience the full spectrum of joy that it was designed to bring into our marriages, but our sexuality is also a powerful, influential force that, when wielded unwisely, can give birth to all sorts of destruction and corruption.

The ripple effect of misused sexuality, and the addiction it can so often trigger, is devastating.

"Do not conform to the pattern of this world,
but be transformed by the renewing of your mind.
Then you will be able to test and approve what
God's will is -- his good, pleasing and perfect will"

Romans 12:2

ACCOUNTABILITY

I don't know if certain personality types are more prone to addiction, but I have discovered in recent years that I'm an all or nothing person when it comes to sugar. And painting my hallway. I may joke about being addicted to tea (and I very well may be...I turn to it when I'm feeling happy, sad, tired, awake, hot, cold or am just in need of comfort), but it is sugar that turns me into a junkie faster than anything I know. While I've tried, over and over again, to enjoy sweets and chocolate in moderation, I've found that I just cannot do it. If I have one Hershey's kiss, I'll have twenty. If I have one brownie, I'll eat half the pan. Until I've grown physically sick from indulgence, my mind will be consumed with covert ways I can walk past the dessert table and snag another one without anyone noticing. I wake up the next morning, head pounding, ears stuffy, throat scratchy, and my heart heavy with guilt over my absolute inability to control myself in the face of sugary treats.

Recent studies have shown that, biologically, sugar actually processes in the brain the same way cocaine does[14].

This sweet poison overtakes me and does me in every single time. I'm the girl who, while making peanut butter fudge and homemade caramels for Christmas, will eat my body weight in samples and will keep putting it in my mouth even *after* the urge to hurl takes over. True story.

In fact, last fall when all the Halloween candy was being

clearanced out, my hubby came home with 4 large Cadbury's mint crème-filled eggs. With the kid's candy bags still bursting at the seams, I stashed them in a bowl out of sight for future enjoyment. A few weeks later I found them while looking for something else and, in excellent sneaky mom fashion, hid my head inside a cabinet and slurped one down. Later that night, after the kids had gone to bed, I practically ran for the bowl. Grabbing a second one, I devoured it with a slightly guilty conscience. *Well, I suppose those were the two parental eggs I inhaled, seeing the kids can't technically split one of these deliciously creamy things.* A few days later, the remaining two caught my eye. *At least the kids will get theirs,* I mused. But in a moment of weakness later that week, I found myself unwrapping and savoring the third egg. Mortified by my gluttonous consumption of the family's chocolate eggs, but very aware of the fact that my hubby had completely forgotten about them and the kids didn't even know they existed, I snatched up the last egg. *Rather remove the evidence completely than have to explain where the other three went,* I reasoned.

I. have. problems, people! I feel completely and utterly out of control when I'm trying to wrestle down my cravings and limit my intake.

My solution? Completely cut it out of my diet. It sounds extreme, I know, and many of my friends and family remain baffled by my ability to sit around a table with them and not blink an eyelid as they chow down on double-chocolate cheesecake.

Last year, in 2013, I gave it up for the new year and was curious to see how long I could go without it. I made it to June 12th. My birthday. In a moment of celebratory weakness, I hollered, "*what the heck,*" sucked down a gooey s'more...and it was all over. Once I had unleashed the beast, there was no going back. I had another, and then another. I'm sure the fact that I'm a recovering perfectionist, who's response to an imperfection in the system is simply *"scrap the whole thing!"* didn't help matters. Once I'd failed, I threw in the towel. I'm working on this quirk, I swear.

For the remainder of the year I fluctuated between abstaining and gorging, and it wasn't pretty. But it was yummy.

So here we are in 2014 and I've given it up again. I don't know when I'll attempt to inch it back into my life, but at this point, I'm loving not being a slave to it.

Few people understand my passionate boycott, but I've tasted crazy, and I've lived with this addiction that literally makes me sick, long enough...and I despise it. The beautiful thing is, once it's out of my system, I don't even crave it. I can stare a triple-layer chocolate cake right in the cherry and say, *"No thanks, baby cakes!"* without an ounce of hesitation. Sure, it looks incredible, and I bet it tastes heavenly, but the feeling of being in control trumps the emergence of that sugar-crazed mad woman any day.

Sugar is my nemesis, and because I've identified the face of one of my greatest opponents, I avoid it at all cost.

Why am I telling you all this? Not because I'm trying to evangelize you over to my non-sugar way of life (although you may be surprised to know that sugar is 8 times more addictive than cocaine[15]...just sayin'), but because this struggle is not unlike our battle with sexually-charged habits.

Just a little taste of sugar, and I was sucked right back in. While masturbation hasn't even featured on my radar for over a decade, the pull of porn occasionally rears its ugly head. There have been times that I've foolishly clicked on a link, or selected a movie on Netflix, that I knew I had no business clicking on -- attempting to justify it to my squirming conscience as a curiosity to know what *"my poor hubby is being tempted with these days."* And just like that, my mind gets snagged on the hook of perversion, and a heavy heart threatens to whisk me into the cycle. *"Gosh, you've blown it now. May as well stick around and play in the mud...you're already dirty,"* the voice whispers.

It happens considerably less often these days, and I bounce back so much quicker, but the temptation is still there.

We are not immune to this disease.

In a survey done by Dirty Girls Ministries, 68% of the women surveyed admitted to using pornography for masturbation, 55% said that their watching of porn felt out of control, and 71% shared that their masturbation behaviors felt out of control[16].

In the same way an overweight person, trying to get a handle on their health, would be foolish to put Mountain Dew and Twinkies into their shopping cart, if you struggle in any of these sexual areas, there are steps you can take to ensure your success in kicking the habit. And much like an alcoholic aligns herself with a support system that holds her accountable and periodically checks in on her, accountability is key.

Over the years, my hubby has met many times with men battling porn addiction, or working through the devastating effects of an affair. I have met with young women trying to turn to God in the midst of their loneliness, rather than to the masturbation and cheap romance novels they've used to try and fill the void.

Why is it that we see accountability as a drag, or a 'necessary evil', when in reality, it's a precious gift and an incredibly helpful tool. I guess it's a matter of perspective.

What's true of penguins and sheep, also happens to be true of humans. Get separated from your flock...and you will not survive. God created us for community for several reasons, and walking through the hard stuff of life *together* is one of those reasons. Accountability provides the perfect means to do this.

If you don't personally have a friend, mentor, pastor or parent whom you can come alongside and request support and accountability from, there are several great organizations out there that offer help. I've listed a few in the resources chapter.

Jim Rohn, a well-known author and motivational speaker, says that "*you are the average of the five people you spend the most time with.*"[17] We often underestimate the impact our social groups have on our decisions. Who you choose to surround yourself with is vital to your success, not only in breaking free of bad habits, but in how you approach the sanctity of your marriage. You become what you behold.

While I'm not saying you should ditch your best girlfriends because they're all raving about their obsession with Christian Grey, it's important that you realize how unhelpful their presence will be in breaking free. Think of it this way: would you rather your husband spend time with other men who are passionate about their wives and families, and who encourage each other in their pursuit of faithfulness and integrity...or a bunch of guys who degrade their "ball and chain," share porn on their smart phones, and constantly invite your man to hit the strip club after work.

Choose your friends wisely. Surround yourself with women who deeply love their husbands, speak positively about them behind their backs, are passionate about personal growth, and who celebrate the gift of marital intimacy.

THE WAR ON SEX

There is undoubtedly a fierce battle raging...and sex is often at the heart of it.

Thieves don't waste time on worthless goods. They go for the most costly, high-profile treasures...and let's just say, the enemy has hit the jackpot.

While uninhibited sexual expression has long been viewed as

natural or normal, study after study is uncovering a dark storm brewing due to our shameless embrace of porn and the adult entertainment industry. Sexual violence is at an all-time high, and we can no longer deny the connection.

It's easy to examine the little we grasp of the sex trafficking industry and label it "bad" and "evil" (which it is), and then, in comparison, label pornography as "neutral" or "harmless." The harsh reality, however, is that they're inextricably connected. As the guys behind the 'Hearts of Men' documentary so stunningly spell out (in exposing the root of sexual exploitation and trafficking), the problem lies in the *demand*[18]. Porn, through the myriad of avenues it's distributed, fuels this demand like nothing else. As long as we're feeding the craving for graphic sexual content, we're fueling the fire of exploitation.

Cut off the root of demand, teaching our kids at a young age to respect and honor the human body, and we might just have the chance to counteract this corruption.

An interesting component of sensuality and desire that is missing from the conversation on sexuality, is the direction in which it should flow. We spend so much time thinking about what we're *getting*, when in reality, we're called to pour ourselves out. Sexual energy is just that, it's *energy*. And where we choose to expend that energy makes all the difference in the world.

We see this play out in the life of King David. The very zeal and enthusiasm that led him to bravely kill the lion and the bear that threatened his father's sheep, also fueled his decision to pursue an affair with another man's wife. The problem isn't passion. It's what we *do* with that passion that matters.

What if, rather than feed our desire and gratify our flesh, we turned that energy into a mighty force of reconciliation and service?

Remember that old Cherokee tale I shared in an earlier chapter about the two wolves? It's the exact same principle in action here. The one you feed grows, and the one you neglect starves.

So, if I may be so bold...what wolf are you feeding, friend? Sexual purity or sexual perversion?

REFLECTION & ACTION:

- How might the choices you make behind closed doors be feeding greed, lies or self-pity?

- Is there something that you struggle with sexually, that you're inclined to hide, and that requires feeding? Is there something you need to lay down?

- What counterfeit have you turned to, to meet a legitimate need for value and satisfaction, that your husband could be meeting?

- In what way could you help protect your heart against temptation?

- In what way could you help guard your husband's heart against temptation?

- How could you *intentionally* fuel the joy, love, hope, humility and purity in your marriage today?

- Begin asking God to protect your marriage, emotionally, spiritually and sexually, and to reveal and restore any ground you may have lost to sexual counterfeits.

"You, my brothers and sisters, were called to be free.
But do not use your freedom to indulge the flesh;
rather, serve one another humbly in love"

Galatians 5:4

15

CHAPTER

DITCH THE CARCASS

While we've experienced a bitterly cold winter season this year, and every third Facebook status update has been a weather-related rant or another expression of disbelief over yet another snow day, it's actually been stunning to experience a fresh, white coating of snow draped over the ground day after day, for almost 3 months straight.

Typically in the heart of winter, we get dumped on, the ground turns white and the trees sparkle like diamonds for two days, everyone smiles, and then everything thaws, the dirty slush gets hurtled onto the white snow by passing cars and we return to our depressing winter pastime of staring out of our fogged up windows at the varying shades of gray and brown until the next onslaught of white wintery weather passes through to deck the ground and make our eyes twinkle. Okay, maybe this is a slight exaggeration of the misery of Michigan winters, but just go with it.

It's the ugly white/brown/gray shuffle that occurs every year. But this one has been different. Even beautifully so.

Apart from the consistently frigid temperatures, which have kept the snow in place, we've witnessed dumping after dumping of fresh snow. There were, at times, drifts so high across the roadways that you couldn't see the houses along-side the road, not to mention the cars hurtling toward you in the other lane.

We have truly witnessed a winter wonderland this year. Along with the extraordinary beauty, has come fabulous excuses to invest in new boots and leg warmers.

And then there are those awkward roadkill sightings. It's comically disturbing, actually.

I recall, after moving to the US as a teenager, being some-what traumatized by the first time I saw a critter get creamed by the car in front of me. But as it turns out, roadkill is simply confirmation that you've crossed over into Michigan. That and the orange construction barrels. Go figure.

So this year, as deer were hit and dragged to the side of the road, they'd promptly get covered up with the next morn-ing's snow. Then as snow accumulated and plows came through and redistributed everything, those frozen deer got hoisted on top of the growing snow pile alongside the road.

I didn't know this was happening until last week, when every-thing started to thaw. I've come a long way since that initial roadkill aversion because apparently awkwardly posed fro-zen deer on top of ice pedestals just do me in. I couldn't help myself, laughter just bubbled out from my warped sense of humor.

These poor deer were grossly hilarious, what with one leg go-ing this way, another going that, and tongue hanging out.

Stick with me, I'm going somewhere with this. I promise.

With the sudden spike in temperature this past week, all the forgiving coverage of the snow-white blanket melted away, leaving behind only the twisted corpses of what had been hiding beneath. What made this sight even more bizarre, was the fact that the cold bodies of the deer had kept the warmth of the sun from melting the few feet of snow beneath them, and so there they sat, hoisted up on crystallized pedestals on display for all to see.

Why am I telling you about dead deer and snow in a chapter about learning to travel light? Well, because I find the parallel startling.

DRAGGING DEATH AROUND

When my family moved to the States in 1997, directly after what I fondly refer to as my "bad year" (because apparently I'm delusional enough to think it only lasted a year), I recall thinking..."*now I can start over. No one has to know what I've done.*" And so start over I did.

I went to a small town high school for my senior year and slowly plugged into a tiny group of friends. With my happy face securely fastened on and my truckload of baggage stuffed tightly away, no one had any idea what kind of life I'd been living just one year prior to that. It worked well for a few years, this little masquerade, because no one was able to get close enough to my heart to prod the tender underbelly of my facade.

It wasn't really until 6 years later, when I started dating my husband, that I was forced to wrestle with the ghosts from my past. I had become so used to dragging secrets, shame and self-loathing around with me that they had become my new normal. All I knew was insecurity, fear and lies.

You see, when I flew away in the Boeing 747 from a homeland that had represented so much pain and perversion, I vowed that I would never let anyone know who I really was inside. I would work to hide her away and recreate the person I desperately wanted to be on the outside.

It's like any big, looming thing that's overwhelming to deal with. We avoid it and stuff it, and I even find myself wanting to do that now when I bump up against things that scare me.

I was so desperate to let go of the ugliness of my past that I distinctly remember doing mental exercises where I would carve out craters in the ground, throw in everything I had done, and then would mentally pour cement over it. I ached to forget. If only I could convince myself those chapters of my life didn't happen, I'd have a chance to move forward.

Forgiveness wasn't really an option at that point because I was quite certain God had fired me. And if He couldn't forgive me, how could I forgive myself?

I had lived a double life for long enough that, while I hadn't given up on Him entirely, I was positive He was done with me. So bringing Him my burdens and baggage didn't seem like a viable coping strategy.

Stuffing, hiding and pretending were all I had left.

But here's where it got scary. I didn't realize at the time that by keeping everything closed away in the dark, I was creating a carnival of chaos for the enemy of my soul. Everything in secret was fair game. I lived in constant fear that if someone found out who I truly was, or what I'd done, I would lose everything. Besides, breaking my parents' hearts, after watching my older sister drag them through something similar, just wasn't an option.

If people really knew me, they'd surely despise me, lose faith in me, and push me away. And I desperately feared rejection and abandonment. So I heaped pretty white snow upon those decaying areas of my soul and impressed people with my happy personality and quick wit. Only, I was *dying* inside.

Literally gasping for air, wondering how much longer I could keep up this charade.

Fear and shame are cruel task masters, and the undealt-with darkness within became the devil's playground. I had worked so hard to convince myself that the previous few years hadn't actually played out the way they did, and seeing no one on this side of the world knew otherwise, putting on a front become my specialty. I began to lose my grip on reality. I started having dreams about being involved in atrocious things, waking up in cold sweats and not being able to distinguish fact from fiction. I felt so incredibly alone during those months because I trusted no one with the broken pieces of my heart, not even the parents I knew loved me so thoroughly.

I had tried so hard to be perfect, and yet in the midst of failing so miserably, had learned the fine art of living two separate lives. I was a great student, a respectful child, a charming friend and faithful pew warmer. At the same time, I had been out drinking every weekend, going home with boys I didn't even know, getting hooked on porn, stealing money from my parents and shoplifting every week.

I got really good at my "that never happened" act over the years, while pressing into every good thing I could. I started leading youth group at our church, occasionally led the women's Bible study, and started working at a Christian Radio Station. By golly, maybe even God was beginning to buy into the act.

Without even realizing it, I was working tirelessly to earn my way back into the Almighty's good graces, never really feeling a connection, because I would never let my guard down long enough to let the good stuff in, for fear that the bad stuff might leak out.

That's the funny thing about locked doors on storage rooms. We may think we can control the exchange of goods, but what was erected to hide the dark parts of our souls, inevitable ends up keeping out the light we so desperately need to work through and release the junk. What was erected to contain the bad, keeps the good out too.

So as my relationship developed with the man I was set to marry -- the second one, funnily enough -- I began to feel the warmth of genuine love and commitment, and those frozen places began to slowly thaw. Suddenly I was scrambling to cover up the unsightly carcasses of what had lain rotting underneath. As the wedding day got nearer, there they were, in all their smelly glory, up on pedestals I could no longer conceal. And I wanted to die.

I could no longer pretend they didn't exist and I could no longer hide the fact that I had lied my way through our relationship in a desperate attempt to not lose the only one I thought would love me through my undeniable brokenness. What I had worked for years to cover up, was slowly beginning to show through, and the fear manifested in a fierce sickness my doctor couldn't figure out. As we wrestled through the muck of my lies and pretense, I was silently fighting with the fear that my promiscuous past had finally caught up with me. Here was God about to sabotage the only good man I'd ever met. Okay, he was just a boy. We were only 21, but we sure felt like grown-ups trudging through this stuff.

As I went through cycle after cycle of antibiotics and plugged in my unusual symptoms into the online symptom checkers, desperate to get healthy before our wedding day, the same diagnosis kept coming up on my screen. HIV.

I knew it. I *knew* it was too good to be true. My iniquities were catching up with me and ol' Jehovah Zapper was gonna get me once and for all. And honestly, it made sense. I'd lost count of the sexual encounters I'd had, unprotected, in a country where AIDS was rampant.

It was time to pay the piper.

But as my parents and fiancé interceded faithfully on my behalf, soaking our relationship in prayer, and as friends and mentors surrounded us with encouragement and truth, my health was completely restored a week before our wedding day and I was left in awe of the goodness of my God.

I share this precursor to my full-blown story (which you'll find in the next chapter), because I believe it's so important that we learn to travel light. We weren't created to lug heavy bags of regret and shame around with us. When our arms are loaded with fear and unforgiveness, there's little room for peace and joy, let alone hope and vision.

And while that's stifling and destructive in its own way, the real danger comes in with the enemy's subtle plot to dismantle our hope. Without hope, we self-destruct. The devil schemes to destroy us from the inside out, and as long as we keep our mask on, no one will know, and we'll slip further into isolation, and desperation.

Transparency and vulnerability are so desperately lacking in this day and age, but every time it's bravely displayed, people are drawn to it.

I believe we're beginning to see through the facade of super-spiritual cookie-cutter perfection, and are recognizing our need and hunger for authentic people. Broken and beautiful.

We are *starving* for authenticity. *Especially* within the church.

If we're willing to courageously embrace our imperfect stories, we'll realize how profoundly beautiful brokenness can be when it propels us into the arms of Jesus. He makes *all* things new.

THE DIFFERENCE IS IN THE DIFFERENCE

It is incredibly important that we understand the difference between guilt and conviction, and between condemnation and consequences.

Guilt says, "*You are bad...you are hopeless...what a foolish girl.*" Conviction says, "*That was an unwise choice, sweet one...but it's not hopeless...let me show you how to fix this foolish decision.*"

The devil specializes in guilt. The Holy Spirit in conviction.

God is so specific when He convicts us of something through the gentle, and yet precise, nudging of the Holy Spirit. He doesn't mess around and He is not a God of confusion. If He wants you to make it right, He'll make it clear and He'll make a way. Your role is to take courage and be obedient.

He is *not* obsessed with our sin (unlike some religious groups often are), but rather He is caught up with life! When Jesus went to the cross for you and me, he took all the punishment of our sin -- past, present and future -- upon Himself. And with this act of radical love, He paid for our sin and we are no longer condemned. While we may get it on one level, when we don't truly comprehend the magnitude of this exchange, it's easy to take the bait when the devil tries to resurrect our past and present it to us as our fallen identity. Christ paid for your baggage completely. Lay it down at His feet and leave it there. Don't allow the enemy of your soul to convince you to pick it back up again. It's no longer yours to take.

With that being said, there are, however, natural conse-quences for the choices we've made and God, being the perfect parent, knows that allowing His kids to experience consequences is one of the most powerful learning opportu-nities we'll encounter in life. While my husband and I no long-er carry the shame and heart-ache from the choices we made years ago, there are still *consequences* we've had to work through, as a couple, because of those choices. God's grace and mercy have lightened the load and enables us daily to learn and grow in the midst of pain, because rarely does He fully *remove* the consequences of the choices we have made.

It may not be comfortable and entirely without pain, but it's never without purpose.

I would urge you to prayerfully look back and, with the help of the Holy Spirit, examine the guilt and shame you might be dragging around behind you. Sexual baggage doesn't unpack itself, it simply slips into the bed beside you and makes connecting with your husband in spirit and truth that much harder.

There are some great inner-healing ministries that help bring freedom in these areas. Search them out and learn to travel light. *It will be so worth it.*

What we believe about consequences, conviction, guilt and condemnation will always reveal who we understand God to be for us. An angry, detached God-figure condemns us and makes us feel guilty, while a loving, gracious, holy God convicts us and allows us to experience consequences while holding us close to His heart.

TRAVEL LIGHT

Just a quick note about forgiveness as we wrap up this chapter about traveling lightly. I truly believe that it is of utmost importance that we learn to process through things while they're fresh, and then let them go. As Ruth Graham Bell so beautifully puts it, *"A happy marriage is a union of two good forgivers."* When we carry unforgiveness in our hearts, be it to someone who wronged us years ago, or towards our husbands who will continue -- in their humanness -- to let us down from time to time, we put ourselves in bondage. Unforgiveness truly is a poison we drink in an effort to wound another.

Be quick in letting people off the hook, including yourself, and remember the incredible debt that God forgave in us. Remember too, that if something has been dealt with and you've told them you've forgiven them, no matter how tempting it might be to beat them with their old baggage, *don't* bring it up again.

Becoming resilient, being quick to forgive, and choosing to not be easily offended are some of the most useful tools you can place in your marital tool belt.

"To be a Christian means to forgive the inexcusable because God has forgiven the inexcusable in you"[1]

C.S. Lewis

REFLECTION & ACTION:

- Are there any secrets you've dragged along inside you, allowing them to quietly destroy your confidence and suck dry your hope? You were not built to carry their load. Offer them up to the One who paid the ultimate price for your freedom. Ask God to lay someone on your heart with whom you could share your heart transparently and vulnerably and start unpacking your baggage with them.

- Have you and your husband communicated openly about your sexual pasts? Is there anything that remains hidden that is causing a disconnect in your intimacy? Ask God to reveal it, uproot it, and reconnect your hearts.

- Is there anything for which you have yet to forgive your-self? When you lay your burdens down at the foot of the cross, your sin is completely covered. All of it. If the Creator of the Universe has released you, who are you to keep yourself captive?

- Is there anyone you need to forgive and release? Ask God to reveal any unforgiveness lingering in your heart, to heal the wound, and then pray blessings over the 'offender'.

"Therefore, as God's chosen people, holy and dearly loved, clothe yourselves with compassion, kindness, humility, gentleness and patience. Bear with each other and forgive each other if any of you has a grievance against someone. Forgive as the Lord forgave you. And over all these virtues put on love, which binds them all together in perfect unity"

Colossians 3:12-14

16

CHAPTER

JOURNEY OF JOY

My older sister and I were born in Cape Town, South Africa, and grew up in Windhoek, Namibia, where our parents moved to a few years later to avoid the discrimination of the apartheid government, among other things. That may sound unusual coming from a white South African, but my parents were passionate about us growing up in multi-racial schools, and felt led to transplant our family in what was then called South West Africa. A few years later, my younger sister arrived, and 3 years after that, our baby sister.

If you're doing the math, yes, that's 4 girls. And a mum. And yes, my dad is a rockstar.

Random fun fact: with my dad also hailing from South Africa and my mom from Zimbabwe, our family of six were born in 3 different countries across Southern Africa.

I have many fond memories of my young childhood, and a startling amount of negative ones. Not because there were more negative than positive, not by a long shot, but because I think that this tends to be the way our brains process life. And the way the enemy of our souls wages war on the battlefield of the mind.

It floors me how, looking back, I can recall things my parents did in complete innocence that were misinterpreted and twisted in my vulnerable little heart. My older sister, with her skinny little body, did ballet. I, however, was "muscular," so I did gymnastics, even though I ached to dance. Sarah, with her beautiful brown eyes, looked lovely in pink, so she got a pink ballerina dress. A blue dress was a natural fit for me with my piercing blue eyes. Sarah's hair was straight and long. Mine, on the other hand, was curly. Only nobody knew this. We lived in a semi-arid desert climate, much like Arizona, which is very unsupportive of follicularly swirly girls. And let me just tell you, if you're going to brush a gal's hair like it's straight -- when it's not -- and *not* give her any anti-frizz serum to make it look good, it is not going to cooperate. And it didn't. My super fine, frizzy hair went every which way, except when we made trips to the coast. Then it curled and looked lovely. Who knew!? So, my mum kept it cut short because it was the only way to manage my mop.

Blue dress. Short hair. No ballet. Large Unabomber glasses. They all spelled out the same thing: *"You are not feminine, Joy, in fact you're sort of like a boy."* It didn't help that I naturally gravitated to the boys, because they were uncomplicated and fun, which further alienated me from the girls. When my body started to do weird things and the boys wondered what was going on, I simply lifted my shirt and said, *"Yeah...check it out...isn't that crazy? I'm sprouting boobs! Wanna touch em?"* I was just one of the boys, and while I loved feeling like I belonged, I ached to feel accepted within my own tribe.

One negative memory can completely obliterate the sweetness of 10 precious moments in our minds. We tend to dwell on and relive the memories that stirred up shame, insecurity, humiliation, discomfort or fear. Maya Angelou explained it like this, *"People will forget what you said, people will forget what you did, but people will never forget how you made them feel."*

And while my childhood was saturated with love and comfort at home, insecurity and self-loathing became second nature during much of my adolescence. I have gaping holes in my memory, mostly between age 8 and 18, where I cannot remember *anything.* It's as if the shame and regret I wrestled with daily blotted out massive portions of my life. The self-hatred made those memories too uncomfortable to recall.

I distinctly remember a recurring daydream I started having around 7th grade. And the dream always unfolded in exactly the same way: me, in all my bespectacled, short-haired clumsiness, awkwardly toeing the cracks in the playground while the popular kids played elsewhere. Some sort of chaos would inevitably break out amongst my classmates and the distinct need for a hero would arise. This is when my fragile heart would practically beat out of my chest in excitement -- it was *my* cue, *my* moment to shine. Even if it was painfully nonexistent.

I would step forward and, reaching around to the back of my neck, would fearlessly unzip the ugliness -- shedding my unsightly exterior, effortlessly stripping away the insecurity and stupidity, peeling back the too-tall, too-thick, über ungraceful facade to reveal the jaw-dropping beauty within. I'm sure she responded to a considerably sexier name. Like Jessica. Or Veronica. Anything but "Joy." Boasting long, gorgeous hair, a tiny waistline, and a beautifully feminine face, she turned heads and won hearts and solved schoolyard problems.

And she was everything I was not.

This was usually where the daydream would end, but it was enough. Enough to temporarily satisfy the ache in my heart.

To be beautiful. To be confident. To be someone other than who I was.

I started snipping diet tips from beauty magazines and compiling health folders before I hit my double-digits. I became obsessed with my appearance, desperate to battle the bulge before it battled me. Watching my mom struggle with her weight for as long as I could recall, and seeing the resemblance in how we were built, struck a fear in me that fueled my obsession.

Despite the lies I believed about my lack of worth and value, I became *that* girl. The one making out with the boys at every middle school dance, not because I really loved to suck face, but because it made me feel pursued and valued, and was, admittedly, rather fun to shock the other girls. I had a new 'boyfriend' every week and lapped up the false sense of confidence it provided me.

While I started to appear happy and confident on the outside, I was empty and broken inside.

My family moved to America near the end of 1994, where I attended my second high school. Talk about culture shock. By the time I had found my feet and nestled into a good group of friends, our visas had expired and we were moving back home to Namibia. With the difference in school year (our school year mirrors the calendar year, while a school year in the States runs from September through June), I begged my parents to allow me to try correspondence schooling, rather than repeat 6 months of school, and struggle once again to fit in with the other kids who'd maintained their friendships in my absence.

The few friends who had stayed in touch with me during my 18 months overseas, via snail mail, were eager to hear how life had treated me. And I was not one to disappoint. I conjured up all sorts of stories about beach volleyball and cheerleading, of which I knew nothing, because the pitiful time I'd spend shuffling through the halls, trying not to be noticed, was too painful to relive. Lying became second nature to me, and with no one to contradict my stories, I simply painted the picture of the life I'd wanted to live. I created the image of the girl I wanted to be, and they bought it, hook, line and sinker.

It seemed, for a time, that life was looking up for me, but the veneer was only paper thin.

After years of childishly dabbling in promiscuity, and yet never crossing the virginity line firmly established in our conservative Christian home, I started dating older boys on the sly. In September of 1996, shortly after I turned 15, I met the sons of one of my dad's colleagues who were visiting from England. I quickly connected with the older one and started spending more time with him. Little did I know of the competition raging behind the scenes in this testosterone-charged household, and the night before their family flew back home, they spiked my drink and the younger one took me downstairs to his room. I don't recall much of the rest of the night, except spending the wee hours of the morning rocking in the fetal position in my older sister's bedroom repeating, "*I'm not a virgin, I'm not a virgin, I'm not a virgin.*" And then there was the phone call I received from a very angry older brother who wanted to know what the hell I'd done with his brother (that I'd refused to do with him) the night before.

I knew little, but I knew enough.

This was a pivotal point in my journey. Life as I knew it had officially changed. The little value I felt I had left had been taken from me, and I suddenly had no reason to say, "no." I threw myself into the arms of any interested male in a hopeless attempt to find significance. I used people and pleasure to temporarily numb the pain, desperately trying to quench my thirst for meaning and value.

Following in the steps of Adam and Eve, I allowed my shame to drive me into hiding, away from exposure and away from God.

The deeper I slipped into promiscuity, the harder it was to get out. Not only was I worthless, now I was dirty.

I jumped from relationship to relationship, going home from the bar with boys I barely knew, often much older than myself. I was only 15, but looked much older, and in a country where underage drinking was the norm and no one was carded, I continued to slip beneath the radar. I had a love-hate relationship with this thing I had going on. I loved the temporary thrill of being pursued, but I hated that it only briefly drowned out the loneliness and isolation. Once over the high, I slipped further into the dark.

"One who is full loathes honey from the comb,
but to the hungry even what is bitter tastes sweet."

Proverbs 27:7

I remember lying dazed in some guy's bed late one night when his housemate returned home. There had been no tenderness, no affection. Only business, without any form of protection. And now, with a third person in the room, there was no introduction. No closing of doors. No respect. Only a sick awareness that I was his prey for the night and the joke was on me. He threw me my clothes and quietly drove me back to the bar where he left me. The next time I saw him was on the rugby field, where I discovered he played for our national team.

You might have thought, by the way I strutted my stuff around town, that I was making a bold proclamation to clear up any doubts about my questionable femininity, *"See people, I have a vagina...and I'm not afraid to use it."* But it was nothing that blatant. Or glamorous.

It was a well assembled front that afforded me the attention I craved, while quietly destroying any remaining shreds of my identity.

I'd nab the boys with my charm and enjoy the temporary thrill of feeling valued. But then it would be time to cough up the goods, and I'd feel stuck. I couldn't escape the hell hole I'd dug for myself, so I learned quickly to run away mentally, while remaining present -- albeit half-dead -- physically. A habit it took me years to break once married.

I was drowning, and no one knew it.

Looking back I've wondered where my parents were while I traipsed around town, wasted and used. But as I get older and wiser, and after several hard conversations with them, I've realized that they were battling their own devils. Knee-deep in good works, they were busy proving their own worth and value, while raising 4 girls.

While my older sister had openly rebelled and fast earned herself the label of 'black sheep', I was still trying desperately to keep my iniquities hidden. I had seen the devastation my sister's exit from our faith had caused my parents, and had determined to not put them through that again. So I was a respectful, hard-working student by day and a faithful pew-warming kid on Sunday mornings...and a bar-hopping floozy by night.

During this same year, I started shop-lifting. It started small, with a lipbalm here or a pack of gum there, and grew to include near daily fixes of clothes, CDs and make-up. Getting things for free became such a thrill, despite the gnawing awareness that what I was doing was wrong, that when I finally committed to stop (years later), it was incredibly hard. Unless you've experience the pull of an addiction, and the cycle of adrenaline and pleasure you experience, it's hard to understand the way in which it sucks you in and then quickly spirals out of control.

I lost two little side-jobs that year as a result of stealing. I even stole several home pregnancy tests that I hurriedly took in grocery story bathrooms, vowing to God that if he would not make me pregnant, I would stop what I was doing. I knew that if that little line were to imply 'with child', that I would be thrust into a new world of scary choices and heart-breaking consequences.

When my parents discovered I had stolen their bank card and had made several withdrawals, and after they'd driven around town early one morning trying to locate me after I'd lied about where I'd spent the night, they knew correspondence schooling had afforded me freedom I had no place managing. Into my third high school I went, where I earned the nickname "the body" and started dating the older brother of a school friend. I kept the fact that he had a son a secret, as I was sure my parents couldn't handle the truth.

More secrets, more separation.

As the crowd I spent time with morphed into a different breed of people, pornography became something I was regularly exposed to. Once again fueling the dump of adrenaline that coursed through my young veins, I got sucked further out to sea.

When we got the news that our visas had been renewed, and that we would be returning to the States, I was all too happy to leave a country that had grown to represent a season of so much guilt and shame.

Two weeks before we flew out, while visiting family in South

Africa, I met a young man. I had just turned 16, and he'd just turned 21. We got hammered, along with 2 others, then went for a joyride out on the town. Trucking down a main street in Cape Town at a ridiculous speed, we hit the broadside of a taxi that had pulled out in front of us. The next thing I knew I was getting a morphine shot in my butt and surgery scheduled for my jaw, broken in two places. You would think that the events of the evening would act as perfectly clear warning signals, but I was too blind to recognize them.

Our relationship continued, long-distance, over the next two and a half years.

I viewed moving across the world as a much-needed fresh start, and I could, once again, present the image of the person I hoped to be. Only this time...one *unblemished* by sexual baggage. I started my senior year at a small town school (my 4th high school, if you're keeping track), and slunk into the background. Sadly, having an accent makes you stand out by default, but with 'insecure' written all over my face, I became prime real estate for those meanies looking for a target.

I had transitioned from a young girl who loved people and thrived in school to a shattered young woman who was afraid of letting people in and who hated the emotional torture of school. I was terrified of my mask slipping, convinced that if anyone knew who I really was, I would be hung out to dry.

While I wasn't physically bullied or tormented, the battle that raged in my head made any encounter with unfriendly people miserable. If someone laughed in the hallway while I was walking through it, they were laughing at me. If more than one person smiled at me when I walked in to the room, it was because I was the butt of their joke. When people didn't greet me in passing, I thought it was because they didn't like me. I longed to be invisible, and yet, watching others blossom in things I was too scared to try out for -- like sports or theater -

- made my heart ache for more. I was desperately jealous of their confidence and courage, but the thought of risking failure was too much to bear.

So I stayed in my shell, dragging my dirty-girl secrets everywhere I went. When my boyfriend would come up to visit, for months at a time, I'd quietly slip back into the lifestyle I'd lived back home, and then seamlessly revert back once he left.

After I had graduated, and while working on my massage therapy certification at the local community college, this boyfriend of mine popped the question. It wasn't really a lovely surprise seeing I'd sort of pushed him into it. I was convinced he was the only one who would ever want me, so I informed him that this was the natural progression of our relationship. I bugged him to hurry up and buy me a ring... while simultaneously insisting that we stop having sex. Not really a good combination for the average male.

God had started to woo my heart and there were certain things I knew I had to weed out of my life in order to get my life back in order.

Little did I know, a new girlfriend had popped up on the other side of the globe -- one who wasn't insisting on a ring or pushing for purity -- and when the email arrived that 18th day of February 2000, informing me that it was no longer working out and that we should go our separate ways, the world as I knew it crumbled. I slept and wept, unable to get out of my bed, spinning that meaningless new ring on my finger.

RENEWED

But this, my friend, is where it starts to get good. The very same week my world fell apart, Jehovah Sneaky was at work behind the scenes. The women from the Bible study that my mum led on a Thursday morning were taking a trip down to North Carolina for a conference. And I just happened to be desperate enough to go with them. While I don't recall too much from the weekend, teaching or ministry wise, I distinctly remember the women who carried me through some of the loneliest days of my life. They scooped me up, lifted my chin, and like a flock of mommas, enveloped me with love.

I spent the next couple of years digging into my relationship with God, avoiding boys like the plague, weaning myself off shop-lifting, and trying desperately to avoid the temptation to slip into the sexual habits I had created years before.

Painfully aware of my inability to have healthy relationships, I told God that my heart was His. Fully and completely. I knew I couldn't be trusted with my heart, as I had flung it at every passing boy over the past several years, so I surrendered that decision to Him, committing to not pursue a relationship again without knowing *He* was releasing my heart into their care.

I started leading youth group, teaching a Bible study, and even stumbled my way into Christian radio. I had started over, stuffed my past down deep enough that it was hardly even discernible, and was now determined to earn my way back into God's good grace. I was going to prove to Him that I was worth saving.

After three years of celibacy, while perfecting my new 'God's girl' image, a pastor I worked with at the radio station introduced me to a young man. While I didn't notice him at first, we kept running into each other at random media events, first at a Michael W. Smith concert, then at a SonicFlood concert, and again at Festival Con Dios. We finally started to connect the dots when the general manager of the station, and our pastor friend, exchanged our emails and got the ball rolling. Because of the hour-long distance between us, we got to know each other via phone and email, and after a month of lengthily conversations, we had our first date.

When I had surrendered my heart to God a couple of years

earlier, I had begged him for wisdom. Having run so quickly into physical encounters with boys in the past, rarely connecting emotionally, and never sharing a spiritual bond, I had asked God to reverse that trend when the man He had for me came along. I watched him honor this request in the following months as we connected instantly over our mutual love for Jesus first, developing a sweet friendship after that, and carefully putting boundaries in place for sexual purity. Everything seemed to be going just peachy!

An interesting thing happened on our second date, however, when the topic of sexual purity arose. Sitting in his Ford Escort in the Farmer Jack's parking lot, I panicked. The conversation had turned to me and I had a choice to make. To tell, or not to tell. Dry heaving out the window, I turned back to him and whispered, *"I was date raped when I was 15."* Nothing more. I had decided to share the 'poor me' part of my story, and keep the 'bad me' portion in hiding, assuming the basic knowledge of me being 'used goods' would vàlidate the presence of some junk to work through.

Heaven knows, if he *really* knew the amount of sexual baggage I came with, he'd head for the hills.

Our relationship progressed and in March of the following year, he proposed in the white sand of a Florida beach at sunset. It was beautiful and glorious, and on that day I was only *slightly* aware of the farce I had become. I had grown so accustomed to pretending that I had almost managed to convince myself that my ugly past was simply a figment of my imagination. I would go through the mental motions of carving out ground at the bottom of the ocean, dumping all my iniquities into the pit, and then smothering them in cement. I would repeatedly drown out the memories each and every time they threatened to rear their ugly heads and remind me of who I was.

From the outside looking in, I had it all. The perfect job, a wonderful family, an amazing fiancé, and impeccable faith.

The only problem was, I knew my life was still a charade, and the fear of exposure -- and the subsequent ruin -- kept me tightly enslaved.

While everything blossomed on the outside, I was quietly withering on the inside.

Secrets will do that to you. I have learned over the course of the past decade or two that whenever I keep dirt hidden, it has power over me. These secrets fester and take on a life of their own, devouring my confidence and joy, and driving me further back into the shadows of insecurity. But when brought out into the light, they lose their power, and I gain power over them. As long as we allow the enemy a foothold in the darkest recesses of our heart, in amongst the secrets and cobwebs, he will poison our self-image, smudge our purpose, and chain us down with fear.

I love the picture painted for us in the story of Rapunzel. Here's this princess, who doesn't even know she has royalty surging through her veins, held captive in a castle she could easily exit, by lies and fear of the unknown. That was my life for so many years. I was utterly terrified of what people would think, of how loved ones would react, that I shoved all my sin and shame into the nooks and crannies of my soul and allowed them to rot. I hoped that if I could stuff it all down far enough, convincing myself that none of it actually happened, who on this side of the world could argue any differently?

This thinking is not only ineffective, but it's about as ludicrous as burying dead bodies in your backyard and thinking their eerie presence won't affect the way you live your life. Garbage stinks, no matter how you gift wrap it, and it needs to be purged. But when your junk is too painful and ugly to even consider sifting through, you get awfully good at holding your nose and stifling your gag-reflex.

I developed such a warped sense of reality that I -- to this day

-- have chunks of memory completely blotted out. I remember several times waking up in a cold sweat from a dream that left me gasping for breath, heart pounding out of my chest. Vivid scenes of my involvement in a murder, and the messy attempt to cover it up. I spent many days searching through my fractured memories, desperate to know whether this was something I had actually been a part of, or whether the devil was simply capitalizing on my inability to separate fact from fiction.

In the months leading up to our wedding, we did everything we knew to do in preparation -- we took every marriage class, read every book, and spent time with older, wiser couples who invested in our relationship. While at times I felt like a fraud in talking about past experiences, simply leaving out *massive* chunks of my history, I had finally managed to convince myself that as long as I could keep up the performance, no one would ever be the wiser. But the alternative was no longer an option.

It was mind over matter, and I was determined to protect this beautiful new life I was living.

Two months before our wedding, in August of 2003, I ended up driving to New York with a close friend for a media event. I assumed it would just be a fun-filled few days at Six Flags, hobnobbing with artists and brushing shoulders with the big wigs of the music industry. But God had other plans.

On the final evening of the event, I found myself sitting front and center in the stadium, media pass hanging proudly around my neck. After Michael W. Smith's set, TobyMac rocked the stage, followed by the delightful presence of Kirk Cameron. I was loving my front row seat, until *she* came out. Pam Stenzel[1], purity advocate extraordinaire. She talked about abstinence and purity and virginity and boundaries, all the things I assumed I didn't really need to hear at that point. After all, I was gettin' hitched in 2 months. She went on to share how important it is to live with full disclosure in marriage, to dialog with honesty and transparency. And I wanted to *die*. I hoped the earth would just open up and swallow me whole. This was *not* what I wanted to hear. After all, I had quietly dragged these secrets around for the past several years, and with my wedding just around the corner, it made no sense for me to go rummaging through the trash now. Let bygones be bygones. Don't stir up this hornet's nest, woman.

But the pit in my stomach deepened as she drove home the need for relationships to be built on foundations of trust. "*Fine, God. Just fine. I get it*" I whimpered. Paralyzed in my seat I watched as people flooded the prayer tent. I was so very aware of an urgency in my spirit, a sense that God was saying, "*Joy, I'm giving you the opportunity of a lifetime...but you have got to act within the lifetime of this opportunity.*" I knew that window would close quickly, as making it to our wedding day without telling him the truth, would mean taking my secrets to the grave. I couldn't possibly burden him with that after he was tied to me.

It was now, or *never*.

The thought of allowing my fiancé into those dark, dirty places of my life seemed impossible, so I thought I'd outsmart God at His own game. "*Okay, God. Let's make a deal,*" I started, "*if I speak to Pam and she tells me I should tell him everything, I'll do it.*" Looking at the growing mass of sniffling bodies in and around the prayer tent, I was certain this was my ticket out. I wandered over, sheepishly standing off at a distance, trying to plan my next move, when I turned to go. Standing *directly* behind me was Pam Stenzel. How He did that, I will never know, but there she was in all her purity-advocating glory, and I couldn't escape. 7 years of running came to a screeching halt and I fell apart in her arms. She cried with me, prayed with me, and confirmed what I felt God was prompting me to do; it was time to take out the trash.

I am so thankful for the precious friend who accompanied me on this trip, a dear friend of my fiancé's long before she became my own. She quietly listened as I processed through my raw emotions, ranging from terror to anger and back again, and then helped me prepare my heart for what was about to take place in my relationship. She, too, prayed with me, encouraging me and speaking hope into my heart, and was the first person to hear snippets of the life I had kept secret.

Once home in Michigan, I went to the apartment we were renting, where my fiancé was currently staying, and waited for him to return home from work. Apart from the day I spent staring at my newborn son through cold ICU glass, being intubated and cardioverted, as medical staff fought to save his life, *this* was the longest day I'd ever known.

After avoiding eye-contact and dancing around the subject for as long as possible, he pried, and I cracked. I don't recall how the words emerged from my lips, but through snot and tears, he heard snippets of a life very different from the one I had painted. Certain the filth of my true identity had manifested on my face, my chin remained planted on my chest as I dredged the secrets up from hiding.

Lies upon lies. Relationship after relationship. Sin cloaked in more sin.

And then he asked me what I feared most he might ask. *"How many were there?"* The number slipped from my lips, and then I was gone.

Convinced this sealed the fate of our relationship, I left my engagement ring on the couch and ran for the bathroom. Curled up in the fetal position on the bathroom floor, I ached for God to just take me home. I was an undone, incoherent and utterly destroyed by my own failed masquerade. Surely death would feel better than this mess I had made.

What felt like hours later, but I'm sure was closer to 30 minutes, I heard him in the doorway. He bent down, scooped me up and, hands firmly holding my face, forced me to look at him. I will never forget the pain I saw in his eyes. *A pain I had caused.* But mingled with the hurt, was a compassion I didn't understand.

He took my hand, got down on his knee, and asked me -- once again -- to marry him.

RESTORED

Oh, friend. This moment will forever be sealed in my memory. Heaven kissed earth in the wee hours of the morning in that little apartment on Potter Street, and through this extravagant expression of grace and forgiveness, that boy changed my life. For the first time, *truly*, in my life, I understood -- tangibly -- the radical love of Jesus. The love that says, "*even though I know you completely -- with all the ugliness and brokenness you carry -- I still want you!*"

I was utterly wrecked in the most beautiful of ways.

The next morning, puffy-eyed and surprisingly courageous, I sat on my momma's lap and told her what had happened back on the night of September 15th, 1996, and how it had impacted the choices I'd made over the next few years. We wept together as she wrestled to understand how they'd missed the warning signs that I was so deeply in trouble. She asked to share it with my dad, and shortly afterwards asked that I share my story with our women's group at church.

Faster than I ever thought possible, this terrible tale that had held me captive all these years lost its power and become a powerful weapon against the very one who had tried to de-stroy me.

The following year, as we navigated the unchartered territory of life as newlyweds, we spoke at a purity conference. Sharing honestly and transparently from our personal journey, we were able to reflect on some of the struggles we were working through as a couple as a result of our poor choices, while celebrating God's extraordinary faithfulness.

And while I'd love to tell you that our life has been sunshine and roses since the truth emerged, we've had a whole heck of a lot to work through.

My husband wisely sought counsel from a Godly mentor. He reminded him how hard it must have been for me to bring this to him, and how important it was that he work through it, forgive me, and then let it go. "*Never bring it up again,*" he added. And I am so incredibly thankful and blessed to say, he *never* has.

While I'm still uprooting lies I believed and associations I made during sexual encounters as a teenager, we've come a mighty long way! Despite the years of junk we've had to wade through, the many soul ties we've had to sever, and the deep insecurities I continue to wrestle with, the sweetness and freedom of our intimacy has grown exponentially over the past several years.

To add to the sexual baggage, I dragged a boatload of emotional wounding into our marriage. I had so cemented into my mind the notion that 'conflict destroys relationships' that it took me years to not shy away from it. Past experience had proven this theory time and time again, so when something was bothering me, I stuffed it. And when my hubby picked up that something wasn't right, and brought it up...I hid.

Fear of disappointing him fueled my drive for perfection and gave voice to my inner critic. The lingering sense that I was never good enough, in the kitchen, bedroom or laundry room, bubbled close to the surface, rearing its head in hypersensitivity and defensiveness.

This poor guy had NO idea what he had gotten himself into.

I cannot imagine what life would be like for us today, had I tried to keep everything locked up inside. I wonder whether we would have even survived. Secrets tend to breed more secrets, which destroy the trust and safety of a marriage, and eventually unravel the very fabric of your relationship.

While those tools we'd placed in our marital tool belt came in handy when dealing with love and respect issues, or gender roles, and finances, nothing could quite prepare us for the daily walking out of married life. Especially one that required much healing and reprogramming for our interludes between the sheets. Our sex life, once settled into, was lack luster at best, as I struggled to stay emotionally present, while shying away from anything creative that might recall the experiences I'd had years earlier. Honest, open discussion, coupled with prayer, really helped us overcome many of these issues, and continues to act as our go-to when, from time to time, unexpected things emerge.

It's been amazing watching God use our journey and our struggles to encourage other couples wrestling with the same stuff. We've had the opportunity to mentor several couples, and lead many different marriage courses, simply because we've made our imperfect selves available to Him, and because we truly love watching our resourceful God redeem our brokenness and use it for His glory.

REDEEMED

We had the opportunity to fly home to South Africa and Namibia in 2006, in celebration of our third anniversary, and to connect my hubby with the family of mine he'd not yet met.

Many of our fondest memories together were created during the 5 glorious weeks we spent gallivanting across the country-side.

On our last evening in South Africa, before heading over to Namibia for our final week of vacation, I had another of those 'God opportunities'. One of those, "*I'm giving you the opportunity of a lifetime...but you have to act within the lifetime of the opportunity*" moments.

We had spent a week with my parent's best friends in Johannesburg and I had been sharing how I was still wrestling with some severe insecurity. In fact, my people-pleaser streak was threatening to become a fully-blown way of life. I was terrified of disappointing people and in my effort to never rock the proverbial boat, I had become relatively passive-aggressive in the way I dealt with things.

My mom's longtime best friend, who had headed up their area's Theophostic Ministry[2] (and inner healing ministry; "Theo" meaning *God*, "Phos" meaning *light*), had asked whether I'd wanted to set aside some time to really pray about these things and ask God what the root issue was. Initially I'd been eager, but as the clock ticked down and our final hours with them became fewer, I felt a mild panic. "*I don't really feel like being an emotional, snotty mess,*" I reasoned. "*Don't worry about it...I'm good.*" But there, in the pit of my stomach, was that bubbling sense of urgency.

Don't miss it, Joy. Don't miss what I have for you.

Just before we were scheduled to be picked up by my dad's sister, who was going to take us to their place, and then drive us to the airport in the morning, I dove in headfirst.

Wait. I want in. I want everything God has for me...bring it on!

So we called and asked her to come 2 hours later, then jumped in with both feet. As I sat cross-legged on her bed, begging God to uproot this life-sucking burden from me, we waited. Allowing God to take me back to the beginning, where lies took root and truths got twisted, the tears and snot began to flow. From the forgotten parts of my heart, God brought to mind snippets of scenes that had taken place when my older sister and I were 4 and 6. He took me, in my mind's eye, to the white garage door of our favorite worker's apartment on the grounds of the hostel we'd lived in. As vice-principle of the high school, my dad also had the position of superintendent of the girls' hostel attached to the school, and it's the place we called home for 4 years after our arrival from Cape Town.

What took place in that small bedroom had been all but erased from my memory. Only fragments had remained, but slowly things shifted into place. Suddenly it all made sense.

All those years I'd wrestled with shame and guilt because something about our childhood had felt mysteriously dirty, but without remembering what had actually happened, I simply stuffed the feeling, owned the shame, and believed that something must just be wrong with me. I was broken. And dirty. And disturbed.

All those years my sister and I dabbled in things we had no place dabbling in. And now it made sense.

This was the missing piece of the puzzle I'd been desperately trying to assemble, and God -- in His sweetness -- had revealed it at the perfect time. The very next day we landed in Namibia, and as we walked the grounds a few days later, hand-in-hand, processing through and releasing the wound of innocence stolen, God brought closure to an incredibly confusing chapter of my life. We stood outside that white door, cried, and let it go.

Upon arriving home in the States, just before Thanksgiving, we discovered we were pregnant with our first child. We did the math and discovered our little lady was conceived in Namibia. How like our God to bring *new life* out of a chapter of my life that had reeked of decay.

We named our daughter 'Alathea Grace', Alathea being Greek for "truth."

For she, our precious gift, was the new life birthed out of a season saturated in truth, and seasoned heavily with grace.

"You intended to harm me,
but God intended it for good
to accomplish what is now being done,
the saving of many lives"

Genesis 50:20

17

CHAPTER

WRAP IT UP

It's easy to wait until your marriage experiences a crisis to spring into action, but having a thriving marriage means doing the work, consistently, and often behind the scenes, on a daily basis.

It means little by little putting things into place before they're ever needed. It's choosing to intentionally stock your marital tool belt with effective tools, carve out time for each other daily, and prioritize your intimacy -- spiritual, emotional and sexual -- when things are going well so that when things aren't, you're prepared.

Oswald Chambers writes in *My Utmost for His Highest* that "we tend to use prayer as a last resort, but God wants it to be our first line of defense. We pray when there's nothing else we can do, but God wants us to pray before we do anything else. Most of us would prefer, however, to spend our time doing something that will get immediate results. We don't want *to wait for God to resolve matters in His good time because His idea of 'good time' is seldom in sync with ours."[1]*

While we often come to God in desperation once things have started unraveling, God longs to be an ever-present source of life, hope and joy in our life, and in our marriage.

Don't be disheartened by the long road ahead, be encouraged to know that we have a great God who is even more interested and invested in our marriages than we are.

Have you ever purchased a jigsaw puzzle that caught your eye with the glossy photo on the box? A magical Bavarian castle, an autumn-kissed landscape, or a basket of fluffy kittens. You brought it home, dumped out its 10,000 pieces, and then promptly wanted to stuff it all back in the box? It can be downright overwhelming to look at the jumbled heap of fragments before you that supposedly come together to create the masterpiece on the box. But remember what your parents taught you? Start with the corners, build the framework, and work your way in.

What we've talked about within these pages are much the same. There are millions of little pieces that make up this work of art, some dark and hard to place, others bright and unmistakable. Each piece is needed to create the masterpiece of marriage and intimacy. Just start with what you know. Get the foundational pieces in place, and then trust your Heavenly Father to help you fill in the rest.

Don't be overwhelmed by the obstacles before you, and don't be discouraged by the current state of your marriage. While big changes and life-altering epiphanies can overhaul your marriage, it's usually the little things, done courageously and consistently, that transform a marriage from the inside out.

You were created for such a time as this, lovingly woven together for a unique purpose, with a God-sized dream buried in your heart. Be true to yourself. Relentlessly pursue wholeness and healing in Jesus, and allow it to overflow into the lives of your loved ones. God's plan for your life -- and your marriage -- is bigger and more marvelous than you could ever fathom.

"Let us hold unswervingly to the hope we profess,
for he who promised is faithful."
Hebrew 10:23

You were born for influence, for authenticity, for impact! You are called and equipped for what lies ahead, but you will need to tap into the endless resources of heaven to realize your potential and step into your destiny wholeheartedly. The more often you turn to Him as your first line of defense, the more natural it will become.

Refuse to allow the storms of life to steal your joy and derail your marriage. Struggles are inevitable, dry seasons are to be expected. But when surrendered to His capable hands, troubled times are redeemed and trials become purpose-filled moments that are transformed into testimonies.

Spiritual, emotional and physical intimacy matter more in this picture than we tend to realize, and we have the Creator of the universe rooting for us. Fight for the unity and intimacy you were intended to experience, and don't allow unrealistic expectations and comparison to rob you of your vision.

Look back only to remind yourself of God's faithfulness. Turn inward when you're tempted to look outward in comparison. Turn outward when you're tempted to look inward in pity. Look upward and remember where your help comes from, and always, always keep your eyes forward, on the finish line. Plant your hand firmly in your husband's, sweet friend, and forge ahead.

You have been made for greatness. Not perfection, but *greatness*. Your marriage was designed to be a trophy of grace, a vessel to display His glory, not through seamless days and smooth sailing, but by simply being an expression of His extravagant love and grace in the everyday.

In closing, I want to encourage you to simply say "yes." "Yes" to an extraordinary marriage. "Yes" to life lived outside the cultural norms. "Yes" to being a catalyst. Where communities are rocked by couples who are committed to walking hand-in-hand, openly and honestly, alongside each other through the beautiful seasons of life, and through the hard.

You, sweet friend, do not have the perfect husband, and you're most likely not the perfect wife. Your home life may not look the way you always envisioned it would, and I can almost guarantee you that your kids don't behave the way you dreamed they would.

Life rarely pans out the way we expect it to.

But if you're willing to step out and say "YES!" to life, using the strength and courage and influence you have today, you have a God who will never leave or forsake you, who's an expert at creating beauty from our ashes, and who will lead you on into a life and marriage more significant, fulfilling and purpose-filled than you ever dreamed possible.

*"I pray that out of his glorious riches he may strengthen you with power in your inner being, so that Christ may dwell in your hearts through faith. And I pray that you, being rooted and established in love, may have power, together with all the Lord's holy people, to grasp how wide and long and high and deep is the love of Christ, and to know this love that surpasses knowledge –
that you may be filled to the measure
of all the fullness of God"*

Ephesians 3:16-19

18

CHAPTER

PRACTICAL IDEAS TO TURN XES AROUND

- Check your price-tag and get your identity and value straight. Ask your doting Heavenly Father to remind you of your true value. When you really grasp how much He loves you, and the price He paid to spend eternity with you, it's hard to stop that radiance and confidence from overflowing into every area of your life.

- Take some time to invest in yourself, pamper yourself, and then set some goals {i.e. put a little more thought into your daily wardrobe, get out and walk daily, eat more healthily, spend more time in the Word allowing God to transform your heart}. The better you feel about yourself, the more apt you are to confidently offer yourself as a gift to your husband.

- Flirt! If the brain is the largest sex organ, and we're slow cookers, it helps to start thinking about gettin' cozy with your man early on during the day. Plan a little. Get creative. And prepare your heart to knock your man's socks off when the opportunity arises.

- Swap 'date night' with close friends every other week so you can get out with your beloved at least once a month. I love that my kids are watching me date their daddy...it models our priorities and expresses the delight we find in our relationship. If finances are tight, have date night at home – but beware, if you're not intentional about putting it on the calendar, it won't happen.

- Invest in your friendship. Make a point of *smiling* at your husband, and find things to *laugh about together*! It's astounding to me how quickly we stop smiling and laughing with our 'forever boyfriends' once the routine of everyday life sets in. Laughter truly is a powerful medicine and it has a mysterious way of knitting our hearts together. Find ways to play together and simply have fun.

- Guard your sanctuary. Turn off the TV in your bedroom (or if you're brave...remove it all together), remove the clutter, dust off the candles and turn your boudoir into a romantic haven for you and your lover. Invest in a good lock for the door if you don't have one yet.

- Just go with it! Don't let your level of interest keep you from engaging. When it comes to women, *desire often occurs after arousal*. Think 'motion activated'. And remember, the more you do it...the more you'll want to do it. I dare you to test that theory!

- Be prepared...if sex isn't messy, you aren't doing it right (stock up: mints, towels, wet wipes, Astroglide, etc.). We keep a little stack of hand towels in my bedside table, and simply restock them once they're washed.

- Plan to escape for a weekend together at least once a year, and grab a local Groupon or hotel deal whenever possible so you can slip away for a night every few months. The change of scenery and removal of distraction works wonders for your chemistry and connection. A hot tub in your room is always a bonus.

- Don't be afraid to get creative. God has given us such freedom in this arena, it is we who tend to put sex in a box and label things as "good" or "bad." There are some excellent books on inspiring creativity in your bedroom, take a peek at the list in the next chapter. For extra fun, go to the link in the 'Printables' section and access your exclusive set of prints where you'll find some sexy love coupons to print.

- Do 'it' first on date night – it's amazing how the dynamic shifts when we slip in a little intimacy *before* date night. Our emotional connection is so much sweeter, it takes the pressure off us in case we're too tired when we get home...and who knows, maybe we'll get to blow their minds with round #2.

- Put it on the schedule. As odd as that may sound, it works. We find time for things that are important to us...but when we fail to plan, we plan to fail. Make it a priority (with a smiley face on the calendar) and that way you always know you'll connect at least once a week when life gets hectic. Go to 'bed' early and enjoy each other.

- Eyes truly are a window to the soul. Be intentional, every day, about making eye contact. Not a passing glance, but a slowing down and zeroing in, allowing your focus to rest on each other's eyes as you shut out the rest of the world. As cheesy as this may sound, we've been doing this for years and it never ceases to amaze us how quickly distraction falls by the wayside when we stop long enough to soak each other in.

- Choose to focus on your husband's strengths and positive qualities. Nothing will squelch the desire to get intimate faster than a foul, negative attitude toward your man. Be intentional about bringing out the gold in him... remember, you have the power to make, or break, him.

- Predictability can extinguish sensuality. Try making love in a new location around the house, or start small and simply get off your bed. It's fun to laugh your way through, *"well, we won't try that position again"* maneuvers in different spots around your room. Make it your goal to 'mark your territory' in every room of the house. And if you're really brave, find a secluded spot outdoors.

- Turn off your phone. With the brilliant technology smart phones have put in the palm of our hands, it's ridiculously easy to unknowingly have a love affair with your phone, while neglecting your spouse. So put the phone down, resist the temptation to check social media every 6 minutes, and enjoy each other in the flesh.

- Learn the fine art of the quickie and establish a signal that you both understand to mean, *"meet me in the bedroom"* (be it a glance or a hand signal).

- Try praying with your husband before intimacy. While it seems odd, it's incredibly powerful. We tend to separate God from sex, which hopefully after reading this book, you'll be less inclined to do. Rather, *invite* God *into* the midst of your passion – it was His idea, after all.

- Invest in a good sound system for your bedroom. I once heard that people who listened to jazz had more sex, and it just so happens we love smooth jazz. Make it a habit to play music and light candles in your bedroom at least once a week, even if it's just to set the atmosphere for cozy conversation.

- Take risks. As you work through any shame or wounding that may have held you back, try bravely offering your body to your husband *without* holding back. Wear something new. Try a new perfume. Shave a different way. Not only will it thrill his socks off, but it'll boost your confidence and elevate your mood.

- Enlist some help! I have a few precious girlfriends who are wonderful at checking in with me from time to time and making sure I've seduced my husband lately. We have great conversations – both inspiring and convicting, but always honoring – about intimacy. We challenge each other onto greater passion. Vulnerable accountability is a real gift in this area.

- Ask God to increase your desire for your husband and to reveal His heart for your marriage. Prayer is powerful. And believe it or not, God wants to increase the passion in your marriage *even more* than you do...and He's wildly resourceful and creative!

"His divine power has given us everything we need for a godly life through our knowledge of him who called us by his own glory and goodness."

2 Peter 1:3

19

CHAPTER

RESOURCES

Okay, so where do we go from here?

While it seems the church has struggled to find its voice in the arena of sexuality, there are in fact some *phenomenal* faith-based resources out there to help increase the sizzle factor in our marriages. I've listed many of them on the next few pages. Keep in mind that while they are from trust-worthy and reputable authors and organizations, you will occasionally stumble upon something that might not sit well with you. Don't freak out, friend. Remember that you and your husband have to find *your own comfort zone* with the vast freedom God has offered us within the realm of creative sexual expression.

I *personally* don't agree with some of the little bits and pieces suggested in a few of the books or websites, but I also realize that it's based on *my preference and my understanding of the topic,* and I refuse to throw the baby out with the bathwater. I choose, rather, to eat the meat and simply spit out the bones, and I would urge you to not choke on them either. We are all so different...and God created us this way. Let's celebrate our uniqueness, not get silly about it.

With that being said, check out this great stuff:

EXCELLENT BOOKS ON MARITAL INTIMACY:

- **Sheet Music**: *Uncovering the Secrets of Sexual Intimacy in Marriage* by Dr. Kevin Leman
- **Sex Begins in the Kitchen**: *Creating Intimacy to Make Your Marriage Sizzle* by Dr. Kevin Leman
- **The Sexually Confident Wife** by Shannon Ethridge
- **The 5 Sex Needs of Men & Women** by Dr. Gary & Barbara Rosberg
- **Red Hot Monogamy**: *Making Your Marriage Sizzle* by Bill & Pam Farrel
- **The Good Girl's Guide to Great Sex** by Sheila W. Gregoire
- **The Act of Marriage**: *The Beauty of Sexual Love* by Tim & Beverly LaHaye
- **Intended for Pleasure**: *Sex Technique and Sexual Fulfillment in Christian Marriage* by Ed & Gaye Wheat
- **Intimacy Ignited**: *Fire Up Your Sex life with the Song of Solomon* by Dr. Joseph & Linda Dillow, Dr. Peter & Lorraine Pintus
- **And They Were Not Ashamed**: *Strengthening Marriage Through Sexual Fulfillment* by Laura M. Brotherson
- **The Sex-Starved Marriage**: *Boosting Your Marriage Libido* by Michele Weiner Davis

- **Sexual Intimacy in Marriage** by William Cutrer and Sandra Glahn
- **Laugh Your Way to a Better Marriage:** *Unlocking the Secrets to Life, Love, and Marriage* by Mark Gungor
- **God on Sex**: *The Creator's Ideas about Love, Intimacy, and Marriage* by Daniel Akin

FAVORITE MARRIAGE BOOKS & SERIES:

- **Sacred Marriage** by Gary Thomas
- **Love & War**: Find Your Way To Something Beautiful in Your Marriage by John & Stasi Eldredge
- **The Five Love Languages** by Gary Chapman
- **For Women Only**: *What You Need to Know about the Inner Lives of Men* by Shaunti Feldhahn (and **For Men Only**)
- **Love & Respect** by Emerson Eggerichs

BOOKS FOR SEXUAL WOUNDING & HELP WITH ADDICTION:

- **Not Marked**: *Finding Hope & Healing After Sexual Abuse* by Mary Demuth
- **The Wounded Heart**: *Hope for Adult Victims of Childhood Sexual Abuse* by Dan B. Allender
- **The Invisible Bond**: *How To Break Free from Your Sexual Past* by Barbara Wilson
- **Beyond Ordinary:** *When A Good Marriage Just Isn't Good Enough* by Justin & Trisha Davis

- **False Intimacy**: *Understanding the Struggle of Sexual Addiction* by Harry W. Schaumburg
- **I Surrender All**: *Rebuilding a Marriage Broken by Pornography* by Clay & Renee Crosse
- **Breaking Free**: *Understanding Sexual Addiction & the Healing Power of Jesus* by Russell Willingham

WEBSITES DEDICATED TO MAKING MARRIAGES SIZZLE:

- **The Generous Wife**: www.the-generous-wife.com
- **The Intimate Couple**: www.the-intimate-couple.com
- **The Marriage Bed**: www.themarriagebed.com
- **Christian Wives Initiating, Valuing & Enjoying Sex**: www.cwives.com
- **Sexually Confident Wives**: www.sexuallyconfidentwife.com
- **Celebrate Your Marriage (Jay & Laura Laffoon)**: www.jayandlaura.com
- **One Extraordinary Marriage**: www.oneextraordinarymarriage.com
- **To Love, Honor and Vacuum**: www.tolovehonorandvacuum.com

BLOGS & COMMUNITIES THAT CELEBRATE MARRIAGE:

- **The Happy Wives Club**: www.happywivesclub.com
- **Time-Warp Wife**: www.timewarpwife.com

- **Women Living Well**: www.womenlivingwell.org

- **The Dating Divas**: www.thedatingdivas.com

- **Fierce Marriage**: www.fiercemarriage.com

- **Simply Marriage**: www.simplymarriage.net

- **Marriage Today**: www.marriagetoday.com

WEBSITES DEDICATED TO SUPPORTING THOSE STRUGGLING WITH SEXUAL ADDICTION:

- www.dirtygirlsministries.com

- www.covenanteyes.com

- www.fightthenewdrug.org

- www.x3pure.com

- www.hopeforone.com

- www.bebroken.com

- www.powertochange.com

- www.xxxchurch.com

- www.heartsofmenmovie.com

TEACH YOUR KIDS ABOUT SEX:

- **Simple Truths** by Mary Flo Ridley (book & teaching)
  www.maryflo.org

20

CHAPTER

PRINTABLES

Download the exclusive set of
Simply Bloom printables,
designed with *your* marriage in mind:

www.simplybloomblog.com/xesbookprints
password: *redeemed*

NOTES

Chapter 1: What Door?

1 I first read about this newlywed couple a few years ago in an online post written by Max Lucado. While I have wildly embellished the original concept, I have traced it back to his book *When God Whispers Your Name* (New York: Harper Collins, 1994)

Chapter 2: Taking Up Residence

1 HELPS™ Word-studies, copyright © 1987, 2011 by Helps Ministries, Inc.

Chapter 3: A Losing Battle

1 Andrew Murray, *The True Vine* (Chicago: Moody Publishers, 2007)
2 This is a phrase used by John Eldredge in *Love & War*
3 John & Stasi Eldredge, *Love & War: Find Your Way to Something Beautiful in Your Marriage* (New York: Random House, 2011)

Chapter 4: The God of Sex

1 Genesis 2:23
2 Nerve Endings: http://www.alternet.org/9-interesting-things-you-may-not-know-about-clitoris
3 Shannon Ethridge, *The Sexually Confident Wife* (New York: Broadway Books, 2008)
4 Dr. James Dobson as quoted by Nate Stevens, *Matched 4 Marriage Meant 4 Life* (Mustang: Tate Publishing, 2011)
5 The concept of teaching our kids to 'manage their freedom' is something we've learned from Danny Silk's incredible book and DVD series, *Loving Our Kids On Purpose* (Shippensburg, PA: Destiny Image Publishers, 2008)
6 Laura M. Brotherson, *And They Were Not Ashamed: Strengthening Marriage through Sexual Fulfillment* (Seattle: Elton Wolf Publishing, 2004)
7 Dr. Dobson as quoted by Laura M. Brotherson, *And They Were Not Ashamed*

Chapter 5: Chasing Extraordinary

1 This story has cycled through the internet and email for years, but I have not been able to track down the source.

Chapter 7: Because Marriage is Just Hard

1 Gary Thomas, *Sacred Marriage: What If God Designed Marriage To Make Us Holy More Than To Make Us Happy?* (Grand Rapids: Zondervan, 2002)
2 This concept of God being more interested in our character than our comfort comes from a teaching I listened to a few years ago by Graham Cooke (you can learn more about Graham at his website: www.brilliantperspectives.com)
3 The story of King David starts with his anointing in 1 Samuel 16 and continues well into 2 Samuel.
4 The story of Joseph can be found in Genesis 37-50.

Chapter 8: At Nascar in a Horse-Drawn Carriage

1 Jill Renich, *To Have And To Hold: The Feminine Mystique at Work in a Happy Marriage* (Grand Rapids: Zondervan, 1975)
2 Gina Parris, *Winning at Romance*: http://ginaparris.com/winningatromance/where-oh-where-did-my-libido-go-%E2%80%93-overcoming-the-pain-of-low-sex-drive/
3 1 Timothy 2:9-11 & Proverbs 31:30
4 Ultimate Orgasm Libido Boosters by Dr. Oz: http://www.doctoroz.com/videos/ultimate-orgasm-libido-boosters
5 Reading chapter 5 (*The Truth About The Way You Look*) in Shaunti Feldhahn's book, *For Women Only* provided much of the motivation behind my desire to tackle this subject of 'the power of the packaging' (Colorado Springs: Multnomah Books, 2004)
6 Matthew 5:27-28
7 Based on a vow Job made with God. This basically means that he's committed to not lust after another woman, to guard his heart, and to be honest with me when he's struggling

Chapter 9: The Truth About Men and Sex

1 Shaunti Feldhahn, *For Women Only* (Colorado Springs: Multnomah Books, 2004)
2 Jill Renich, *To Have And To Hold: The Feminine Mystique at Work in a Happy Marriage* (Grand Rapids: Zondervan, 1975)
3 Dr. Laura Schlessinger: http://www.drlaurablog.com/category/today-show/ (March 28, 2008)
4 Dr. Daniel G. Amen, *Sex on the Brain*: 12 Lessons to Enhance Your Love Life (New York: Random House, 2007)
5 Gary Thomas, *Sacred Marriage: What If God Designed Marriage To Make Us Holy More Than To Make Us Happy?* (Grand Rapids: Zondervan, 2002)
6 C. S. Carter (1992). Oxytocin and Sexual Behaviour. Neuroscience and Bi-obehavioural Reviews, 16(2), 131-144 (http://en.wikipedia.org/wiki/Sexual_motivation_and_hormones)
7 This fabulous terminology comes from Bill & Pam Farrell's book, Red Hot Monogamy (Eugene, Oregon: Harvest House Publishers, 2006)
8 Mark Gungor, *Laugh Your Way to a Better Marriage* DVD (Crown Comedy, 2009), watch an excerpt here: https://www.youtube.com/watch?v=TbJOL0X4PXA

Chapter 10: Honey, I Have A {Life}

1 Michele Weiner Davis, *The Sex-Starved Marriage: Boosting Your Marriage Libido* (New York: Simon & Schuster, 2004)
2 Newsweek Cover, June 30th, 2003: http://www.prnewswire.com/news-releases/newsweek-cover-no-sex-please-were-married-71373437.html
3 Family Circle Survey Link: http://www.familycircle.com/health/emotional/self-improvement/family-circle-survey-mom-confessions/?ordersrc=rdfc1108470#page=3
4 Patricia Love, *The Truth About Love: The Highs, The Lows, and How You Can Make It Last Forever* (New York: Simon & Schuster, 2001)
5 Gary Thomas, *Sacred Marriage: What If God Designed Marriage To Make Us Holy More Than To Make Us Happy?* (Grand Rapids: Zondervan, 2002)

6   Bill & Pam Farrell, *Red Hot Monogamy* (Eugene, Oregon: Harvest House Pub-
    lishers, 2006)
7   'P=p-i' is attributed to Tim Gallwey (www.theinnergame.com)

Chapter 11: Stop, Drop and Roll

1   Emerson Eggerichs, *Love & Respect: The Love She Most Desires, The Respect
    He Desperately Needs* (Nashville, Thomas Nelson, 2004)
2   Shaunti Feldhahn, *For Women Only* (Colorado Springs: Multnomah Books,
    2004)
3   Proverbs 18:21
4   James 1:19
5   Colossians 3:13
6   1 Corinthians 13:5
7   Gary Chapman, *The Five Love Languages: The Secret to Love that Lasts*
    (Chicago: Moody Publishers, 2009)
8   Afrikaans for "speak the language"
9   The idea of 'digging for gold' in others comes from the brilliant Bill Johnson
    (Bethel Church, Redding California)

Chapter 12: The Joy Thief

1   Nonverbal Communication: http://www.nonverbalgroup.com/2011/08/how-
    much-of-communication-is-really-nonverbal/
2   Kris Vallotton is one of the pastors at Bethel Church in Redding, California
    (www.kvministries.com)
3   Steven Furtick is the founding pastor of Elevation Church in Charlotte, North
    Caroline (www.stevenfurtick.com)
4   Jon Acuff, Quitter: *Closing the Gap Between Your Day Job & Your Dream
    Job* (Brentwood, TN: Lampo Press, 2011)

Chapter 13: Spirit Mingler

1   Howard Thurman (1899 – 1981) was an influential African American author,
    philosopher, theologian, educator and civil rights leader.
2   Gary Thomas, *Devotions for a Sacred Marriage* (Grand Rapids: Zondervan,
    2005)
3   Genesis 2:24
4   Cleave – to adhere: http://Biblehub.com/hebrew/1693.htm
5   This phrase comes from *Love & War* by John & Stasi Eldredge
6   Adam & Eve: Genesis 2
7   Jesus & the Church: Revelation 19:7-9
8   John & Stasi Eldredge, *Love & War: Find Your Way to Something Beautiful in
    Your Marriage* (New York: Random House, 2011)
9   You'll find a lovely tribute to the legacy of Ruth Graham Bell here:
    http://billygraham.org/decision-magazine/june-2013/ruth-bell-graham-a-life-
    well-lived/
10 This concept of God being more interested in our character than our com-
    fort comes from a teaching I listened to a few years ago by Graham Cooke
    (you can learn more about Graham at his website:
    www.brilliantperspectives.com)

Chapter 14: Fifty Shades of Counterfeit

1 5 Brain Chemicals in Healthy Sexual Act and How it is Different from Pornography Addiction: http://www.feedtherightwolf.org/2010/11/brain-chemicals-in-healthy-sexual-act/
2 Covenant Eyes Porn Stat Report: http://www.covenanteyes.com/pornstats
3 Click on the 'marriage' tab: http://www.covenanteyes.com/pornstats/
4 Your Brain on Porn: http://yourbrainonporn.com/erectile-dysfunction-porn-part-1
5 How Porn Ruins Your Sex Drive: http://www.covenanteyes.com/2010/01/25/how-porn-ruins-sex-drive/
6 From a testimony on the effects of pornography given before a U.S. Senate Sub-Committee on Nov. 9, 2005, by Jill Manning, a sociologist at Brigham Young University: http://www.fathersforgood.org/ffg/en/month/archive/oct08/testimony.html
7 3 Reasons to Beware of Porn (Porn Fails to Satisfy) by Mark Chamberlain, Ph.D: http://simplemarriage.net/3-reasons-to-beware-of-porn/
8 1 Corinthians 6:19
9 1 Corinthians 7:4
10 Masturbation, The Secret That Ruins Great Sex: http://www.freedomeveryday.org/sexual-addiction-articles/viewArticle.php?articleID=83
11 Helen Keller, The Miracle Worker: Selected Works of Helen Keller (Createspace, 2011)
12 BDSM is a variety of erotic practices involving bondage, dominance and submission, role-playing, and sadomasochism (to name a few).
13 Mark Gungor, Laugh Your Way to a Better Marriage DVD (Crown Comedy, 2009)
14 www.nydailynews.com/life-style/health/researcher-sugar-addictive-cocaine-obesity-diabetes-cancer-heart-disease-article-1.1054419
15 Dr. Mark Hyman, M.D.: www.nydailynews.com/life-style/health/white-poison-danger-sugar-beat-article-1.1605232
16 Christian Women & Porn Addiction : http://dirtygirlsministries.com/wp-content/uploads/2014/02/DGM-Addiction-Infographic-2014.pdf
17 Jim Rohn was an American entrepreneur, author and motivational speaker (www.jimrohn.com)
18 Unearthed: Hearts of Men (www.unearthedpictures.com)

Chapter 15: Ditch The Carcass

1 C. S. Lewis, The Weight of Glory (New York: Harper Collins, 2001; Originally published 1949),

Chapter 16: Journey of Joy

1 Pam Stenzel : www.pamstenzel.com
2 Theophostic Ministry is a powerful inner-healing ministry based on uprooting lies from our past, founded by Dr. Ed Smith (www.theophostic.com). Another wonderful ministry is Sozo through Bethel Church (www.bethelsozo.com)

Chapter 17: Wrap It Up

1 Oswald Chambers, My Utmost For His Highest (Uhrichsville, OH: Barbour Publishing, 1963)

ACKNOWLEDGMENTS

My humble gratitude goes out to:

Joe, my beloved partner in crime, without you I would have had no reason to write this book. The love, grace, passion, faithfulness, integrity and wisdom you offer on a daily basis astound me. Thank you for fueling me with hot beverages and graciously accepting the obvious lack of clean underwear and socks while I wrote my heart out. You rock my face off, I adore you!

Mom and dad, what an honor it is to be your daughter. Thank you for blazing a trail of hope and leaving a legacy of love (and for setting the standard so high...one day we'll beat you). You inspire me more than you'll ever know. Thank you for faithfully cheering me on. I love you so much.

To my beloved girls: Cynthia, Bethany, Rachel, Melissa, Amanda & company. Your friendship delights my heart, fuels my love for Jesus, and celebrates the beautiful complexities of marriage...what more could a girl ask for in her friends?

Ashley Wells: thank you for the tremendous role you played in bringing this dream to life.

Heidi Short: thank you for making me sound more acceptable than I actually am. What a blessing you are!

To Order More Books:

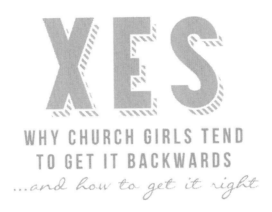

XES

**WHY CHURCH GIRLS TEND
TO GET IT BACKWARDS**

...and how to get it right

IS AVAILABLE ON
AMAZON & KINDLE

SHARE YOUR THOUGHTS ABOUT THE BOOK
OR REQUEST INFORMATION ABOUT
HAVING JOY SPEAK AT YOUR NEXT EVENT:

joy@simplybloom.org

STAY IN TOUCH:

www.simplybloom.org
facebook.com/simplybloom

ABOUT THE AUTHOR

Joy McMillan is a freelance graphic designer, writer, conference speaker, and tea drinker extraordinaire. She is the founder of Simply Bloom Productions LLC, a creative little company with a big heart and an even bigger dream.

Joy & Joe have been involved in leadership & marriage ministry for as long as they've been married (2003), and with one foot planted firmly in the law enforcement world, they feel a tremendous burden to champion and celebrate God's passion & purpose for marriage.

Originally hailing from Southern Africa, Joy lives with her scrumptious husband and two beautiful loin-fruit in Michigan.

Made in the USA
Charleston, SC
15 September 2014